BEAUTY & THE BEST3

22 Stand Out Leaders
Share Their Experience, Challenges
And Best Advice For Achieving Success
In The Beauty Industry

Edited By Susan Routledge

WM

Beauty & The Best 3

First published in August 2025

Available in Pbk 978-1-917265-51-5

W&M Publishing

A CIP catalogue record for this book is available from the British Library.

Contents

Welcome to Beauty and The Best 3

Coming together is a beginning;

Keeping together is progress;

Working together is success.

I love Henry Ford quotes and this has to be the quote that gels together all three of the *Beauty & The Best* books along with the whole of the incredible Beauty Industry.

I believe that the beauty industry is far more than just an industry; it is a living, breathing, ever-evolving community built on creativity, care, and an unwavering passion for helping others feel their very best. From the smallest treatment room to the grandest spa, every corner of this industry holds a story – and behind every story, there is a person with a dream, a vision, and the courage to make it a reality.

The timing of *Beauty & The Best 3*, four years after the release of the other two books seems such perfect timing as inspiration in the ever changing world of business.

It features 22 exceptional business owners who came together as members within my Beauty Directors Club. These are fantastic individuals that I have had the privilege of working alongside, and watching flourish, whilst each on their own unique journey.

Their businesses may vary in size, style, and location, but they are united by following their dreams and their resilience, their innovation, and their deep care for both their clients and their teams.

What makes this and our other editions so special, is the honesty. These are not glossy tales of overnight success. Instead, they are heartfelt, genuine accounts of determination, setbacks, breakthroughs, and the priceless lessons learned along the way.

Each author shares their challenges as openly as their triumphs, proving that even in the face of adversity that passion and perseverance can create something truly extraordinary.

The Beauty Directors Club was founded with one core belief: that when passionate, driven people come together to share their knowledge and to support each other, that the impossible becomes possible.

The authors in this book embody that belief every single day. They have poured their hearts into their chapters—not just to tell their stories, but to inspire yours.

On behalf of all of us, I hope you find inspiration in these stories—whether you are a fellow beauty professional, a loyal client, or someone dreaming of starting your own journey in this incredible industry.

May these chapters give you hope, encouragement, and a continued belief in your own potential.

Susan Routledge

Star Gazing Amongst Shooting Stars

Susan Routledge

I don't think I ever imagined that I could have the life I lead, doing what I love, surrounded by the most awesome people, and to get to call it my career. It's a life I love, and I am so grateful each and every day.

I wrote my first chapter in *Beauty and The Best 1*, all about my start in the beauty industry and building my own beauty clinic which is now celebrating it's 37th Anniversary. I called that chapter 'Reaching for the Stars'. The beauty industry has always been the only industry I ever wanted to work in, and I love the constant choices and opportunities that it allows, both myself, and others, from so many angles.

I now feel that I have the absolute privilege to be the star gazer watching and helping the most inspiring entrepreneurs literally turn into shooting stars by reaching new heights both personally and within their businesses, whether it's growing from new opportunities or achieving accolades and awards.

My clinic is ran by the most amazing and fabulous team, who continue to elevate our reputation, and who work consistently with our fantastic clients, some who have been with us since day one.

This gives me the freedom to help other salon and clinic owners to develop their businesses to ultimately fit in within their lifestyle needs and wants. I always say 'Your Business, Your Rules' and I truly mean that. My other saying is 'You are not your business, but it has to be your very lucrative, supportive and profitable friend'.

These two principles are non-negotiable to me.

Business should be fun, but it can so easily take over your life. I see it happen so many times, where I watch burnt out entrepreneurs making themselves ill in the pursuit of so-called 'Success' portrayed mainly by others on social media, who aren't necessarily being truly honest.

Success comes in so many forms. Yes, of course money is important, but without health, joy, lifestyle and fulfilment, then money is worthless.

I learnt this lesson early on in my life when my Dad suddenly passed away at only 50 years old. He was working 14 plus hours a day, for his ultimate goal which was to make enough money and passive wealth to retire at 55.

Did the crazy hours he worked contribute to his shortened life? We will never know. What I do know though is that I saw it hugely impacting, relentlessly on his stress levels and his family life. I also know that although I would give anything to have my Dad back, his passing taught me one of the biggest life lessons in the most unforgiving way.

So after building a cupboard full of National business awards, I stepped away from working in the treatment room to help others to build their businesses to be so robust, that it will be consistently successful, but always with the freedom to be on their terms.

After years of 1-2-1 salon business consultancy, I realised that I had a unique formula, that I was naturally teaching, based on strategies I had learnt from spending a year closely shadowing a business mentor who specialised in business mergers and acquisitions. I found that my formula for success, worked on any size business and gave the owner the ability and choice on how to command their profits, on their terms, in a business that worked for their lifestyle.

In 2016, I trademarked my S.T.A.B.L.E formula and I turned it into a six month online programme. The anagram stands for Systems, Trust, Adaptability, Brand & Education used within five key areas of a business. Cash, Clients, Assets, Team and most importantly YOU as the business owner.

By 2018, the success of the programme and the businesses who had completed were all fully thriving, but something was missing, I had no support mechanism to further support these awesome entrepreneurs to continue developing, which saw the birth of Beauty Directors Club and this is where my new chapter truly starts.

I officially launched Beauty Directors Club at Professional Beauty, ExCel in London at the end of March 2018. I knew exactly what I wanted to launch, but didn't really know how to get that message across. I knew I didn't want to have just a standard membership for salon owners but if I'm truly honest, that was what I had created.

The launch was a huge success and I had so many members joining, but something was missing and I couldn't put my finger on it. I really thought I had created a monster. I had lots of members joining and also lots leaving too. It was like a revolving door, but through that door, I could also see some of my ideal members, ones that resonated perfectly with what I was trying to create. By the start of 2020 things had stabilised, and I was only attracting my dream members.

These were established beauty salon and skin clinic owners, all wanting to work to the highest of standards. I wanted to create a safe, confidential community, where there were no ego's and the best support network, where everyone was treated the same, whether you were a solo operator or a multi-site business owner. I had also attracted a network of fantastic expert business mentors who could offer help and advice to my members in the areas that were not my strengths. I always believe that you should never profess to be an expert or teach topics in anything that is not your full time career, so I introduced experts from finance, marketing, HR, Law so we had a cocoon of support from true experts in each area.

Things were ticking by nicely, and I had some writing I needed to get done so I decided to head off to Thailand in early March 2020. The idea was that I would go out, get my work done and then Stephen, my husband would fly out a week later so we could both have a lovely break and fly back together.

I can distinctively still hear Vicky, one of my head therapists who never misses the news, saying to me 'I think this Coronavirus might be big. Are you sure about going to Thailand?' I'd only heard it mentioned once before so I replied 'Yes, it'll be fine' and bags packed, off I went.

It truly was fine out there. I had no TV, and just snippet updates from calls to the UK. It was only when Stephen told me that with less than 24 hours notice that his flight was cancelled that I thought things might be changing but I told him to book an alternative flight. Things then suddenly started to change in the UK and there was talk of a lockdown. It really was still another world in Thailand.

The only restrictions were that you had to sit down to eat, and you couldn't drink alcohol after 9pm. There was no panic buying of food, and no toilet roll shortage either !!

I firmly believe that I was meant to be there, because away from the panic, I could be far more useful to my clinic team, my Beauty Directors Club members, and to the Industry in general. I had the time to source the best information, and managed to find experts to talk about furlough schemes, insurance, hygiene, business help etc. So I started daily live interviews on social media. We sometimes had more than 400 on the lives with everyone scrambling for the best help.

Stephen and I managed to get the second from last flight back to the UK on the 26 March to a whole new world.

This was when I became truly aware of the strength of Beauty Directors Club, together we were so strong. I have never seen such resilience and camaraderie build so quickly. Whilst there was fear and panic out there, we stayed so strong, with constant sharing of knowledge and an inner warmth that I have never ever thought I could experience from a group of virtual strangers coming together to be the best of friends and allies.

That strength has never faltered and it brings me to near tears of pride every time I think about it.

Although those were tough times for everyone, we stayed strong with different fun challenges and this is originally where the idea for the Beauty and the Best books came from. These books have been used world wide to inspire others, and we are so proud that companies such as Phorest Salon Software use them as part of their induction process for new team members to understand their clients.

During lockdown we also had a new member join us from

Malta and we lightheartedly used to joke that we would all land over there, but in true BDC manifesting style, the Maltese government were encouraging travel with some great incentives. So in January 2022 over 40 members and partners headed to St Julians Bay for the first of our annual BDC Malta Business Bootcamp events. We now have great bonds with salon owners in Malta who spend time with us when we are there, and also now come to the UK Trade shows.

We also decided we needed a large challenge to work towards, which then prompted the start of a three-peak mountain challenge, starting with Mount Snowdon which we climbed in the dark with head torches, just to add a bit more excitement. What I love about these challenges is that out of the 34 who climbed only two had ever attempted mountains before. What I also love is that we also always had our BDC cheerleaders who are members who don't climb but just want to soak in the fun atmosphere of when we are all together. It is truly magical.

From there we also raised money to give interest free business loans to female entrepreneurs in developing countries to start their own beauty and hair salons so they can support their families. We have also donated and supported the Hair & Beauty Charity too.

All of this positivity has also led us to host networking events called Beauty Round Up within Professional Beauty Shows and now beyond, where we highlight some of the amazing business models from BDC.

I also now I have a podcast called Beauty Business Matters where again, I highlight great business with weekly interviews from the good and great from our Industry. The podcast hit

No 3 in the UK as soon as it was released and has already hit over 50 episodes and over 5000 downloads.

So what's next? Well, we will continue to steadily grow Beauty Directors Club which is currently only waitlist, recommendation or invite only. I am also taking the network events out across the UK, and I am also releasing some new in-person national events too.

I truly love being a star gazer, as our industry has the best shooting stars, and I feel so privileged to get to work alongside so many fantastic entrepreneurs, and to fire some rockets of desire amongst them. I really do hope this chapter, and every page in this book inspires you to reach for your stars.

Anything is possible.

Keep shining !! x

Susan Routledge – Founder of Beauty Directors Club

Susan Routledge is a Multi Award Winning Salon Owner, International Business Consultant, and trusted Industry Advisor.

Susan founded her clinic 37 years ago and it's remains the largest independent beauty salon in the Northeast of England.

She is also one of the Board Directors for BABTAC representing Industry Standards. Susan is also one of the experts on the Advisory Panel for the PHAB Service Stars and she also sits on the committee for The Hair & Beauty Charity

Susan is the creator of the exclusive Beauty Directors Club.

She also has a trademarked business formula utilised in her two online business programmes.

Her down to earth, light-hearted approach has made her an International Speaker and a long established Awards Judge.

Susan also hosts networking and business education events, highlighting successful business practice.

Most recently Susan has launched her podcast called Beauty Business Matters where she interviews top CEOs and beauty professionals

The podcast reached No 3 nationally, and has currently had over two million views on Facebook.

https://susanroutledge.com

https://beautydirectorsclub.com

The Power of One 'YES'

Andrea Simpson

I remember walking into ESPA House on a beautiful warm Friday afternoon and took a breath ... the energy I felt at that moment was captivating almost enchanted. As I climbed the stairs I was fascinated by the 'cloud like' lighting that cascaded from the ceiling, it was like it was beckoning me to a magical world beyond ....

As I left, what I call my 'Opportunity of a Lifetime' interview, Marian the Director of Training walked me to the door and said, "I want you to think long and hard about everything we have talked about and I will call you Monday."

That 'YES' changed everything for me. Not only as a therapist and educator but as a woman in her 40's, at a point in life when we start to view ourselves differently. That very important (and scary) 'YES' paved the way of how my career would evolve. Over the years it would give me challenges that raised anxiety, highs that took my breath away, solo travel globally and a journey of self-discovery. I will always be eternally grateful to Marian for seeing that 'something' in me, for the opportunity that changed everything. Without that 'YES', I wouldn't be here writing this now.

Destination: Beauty

When I served in the British Army, at the age of 18 my first posting was to The Joint Headquarters British Army of the Rhine (JHQ BAOR), Germany. Within a year or so, of being there, a detachment tour to the Falkland Islands arose and my 'YES' hand of opportunity waved in the air.

That was back in 1987, not long after the Falklands war. The military gave me so many opportunities to say 'YES' to be pushed out of comfort zones and to experience many things. I skied, I parachuted, I ran, did charity mini-bus pushes, Northern Ireland Training and even had chance to drive a Challenger tank on the muddy tank ranges in Germany. I could (I should say "had to') strip down, clean and reassemble weapons like the Self-Loading Rifle (SLR), Submachine Gun (SMG) and pistol, under timed pressure testing too.

Throughout the military, beauty was always there. I cleansed, I moisturised, I used eye cream from the age of 16. I had a Phillips face steamer my flat mates used to borrow and a dear friend who I joined the Army with in '86' (we are still friends to this day) told me a couple of years ago she has moisturised her skin every day since I told her so way back then!

After my son was born, I went back to college fulltime to study NVQ Level 2&3 Beauty Therapy. Since that day I have never worked a day. I make no apology for being a self-confessed and madly obsessed skin geek who loves to fuse my love of skin science, sprinkled with my other love of gentle, intuitive ayurvedic principles.

Whilst completing the Level 3 Beauty, Electrical Route, I was hooked on Anatomy and Physiology, finding it fascinating and was always wanting to know more. I loved using all the facial machines, layering and combing them to make bespoke skin treatments. I just couldn't get enough of facials. I made a conscious decision then (and manifesting) that at some point, all I wanted to do was facials. It was my happy place.

It's on reflection now, I can now see that was the beginning of my journey specialising in facials and skin. I was awarded Student of the Year at college. At that time Dermalogica gifted a year of free unlimited Education Courses at the International Dermal Institute. I did every single course they did, soaking up all the skin science I could! Never for a moment did I think then, as I write this, that just a few evenings ago would be sat at dinner again with Candice Gardner, the Education Manager for Dermalogica and the other co-authors, editor and publisher reminiscing this story and how that invitation to education by Dermalogica, influenced my path to becoming a facialist.

As my early career picked up pace, I loved feeding my brain and heart with the beauty industry. I worked for the 'best, award winning and recognised salons and spa's I could. Weekends, bank holidays, late finishes, early starts just rolled on, learning my craft from very successful businesses, their client journeys and how they implemented impeccable attention to detail and importantly, time management of a day back-to-back with guests and clients.

I said 'YES' to every training opportunity that came my way with brands, techniques, equipment, products and took on responsibilities where I saw opportunities to advance and learn more. Too often now I see therapists wanting to specialise too quickly. My advice? Slow down!

The broader the knowledge in the industry, the better treatments can be given, technically and safely and you really begin to understand where your calling is and master it with expertise.

Saying Yes When It's Easier To Say No

Around 18 months ago, I lost my lovely mother-in-law. That same week, I was climbing into my (non-negotiable) daily ritual evening bath, when my phone bleeped with a txt message from Joan Scott, the CEO and Chair of the Hair and Beauty Industry Association (HABIA) … she was pulling together successful people, to write a book. It was going to be called 'Leading from the Heart' and she wanted me (I still to this day can't believe it) to contribute to the book. I didn't hesitate for a moment, pinging back straight away "YES … I am in!"

The deadline was tight, my work diary was packed, my husband had lost his mum and the only window of opportunity I had to write my chapter was four hours the day after her funeral. I hit the 5pm deadline with half an hour to spare if I remember rightly. I honestly can say I did wonder, as I sat down to write that lunchtime, why I said yes. I am glad I did. Despite the timeline and circumstances, I had to deliver the copy, I achieved it and recognise again, the challenge was meant to be accepted. It wasn't perfect, but it was honest and I showed up and kept my promise. Saying 'YES' lead to contributing to another Global Best-Selling Book this year called 'SHINE'.

Building A Brand With Soul

When I founded my business at the beginning of 2019, it was another one of those moments in my life that was meant to be. I had recently left my role as Training Manager for the America's and the Caribbean and was taking a walk one grey and damp Sunday afternoon with my husband in a beautiful village, not far from where I live.

Tucked away, on the corner of the high street, I spotted an old cottage, that was a children's shop.

It was full of clutter, the exterior worn and I wondered why I had never noticed it before.

Crossing over the road, I peered in through the window and my heart skipped a beat. I turned to Mr S and said, 'this would be perfect for me'. Turned and walked on. I remember feeling sad because retail property rarely came available in that village.

That was the Sunday... on the Friday, a few days later, I was scrolling through social media and let out the biggest scream! (nearly spilling my tea). I ran down the stairs to Mr S, shouting (possibly screaming) "OMG, you won't believe this, you won't believe this!!!" The little children's shop had come available to let!

It was 7.30am in the morning: I text the mobile number 'I know it's only 7.30am, I can't wait for the office to open at 9am, I want to be the first to see this!'

My phone rang five mins later, it was the agent. I had viewed by 9.30am. I struggle to verbalise the feeling that overcame me when I walked in the doo... it was like a welcome home hug that had wrapped itself round me. I said YES! Went home and said to Mr S, you had better come and look at this. I had the biggest smile.

I do believe that little building was waiting for me to love and care for it. That Sunday, as I peered in the window, I think I made a little wish, putting energy out to the universe or maybe a little bit of manifesting? Whatever it was, as I opened the door on my second visit that morning, sat on the old oak step was a wooden sign: It read "Dreams really do come true". That little sign still sits there today, the lady of the children's shop gifted it to me, saying 'you're meant to be here.'

That same day, I sat with a blank piece of A4 Paper. In the very centre I wrote

'It's never just a facial …' circled it with a roughly drawn heart. Those five words are so precious to me.

They capture energy, expertise, results, ambiance, feelings, technology, touch, aroma, mindfulness, awareness, care, empathy, experience, life, love and that 'just something' that you can't quite explain or define, that makes a facial so much more.

Those words are the heartbeat for every treatment, for every business decision I make, for those little subliminal touches, for brands I work with and for the experts I collaborate with, those 5 little words are etched in everything I do.

Because they are so important to me and the foundation of everything about my business, I had to protect them. My clients quote the words most days post treatment, on their testimonials and tag them on social media posts. The only way I could treasure them, was by trademarking them, which I did.

I believe by trademarking 'It's never just a facial®' strengthens the deep belief in what I do, it's good business acumen, values my own worth, owns my own voice and protects what I have created.

Reflections

"Say YES! …You will figure it out afterward".

Tina Fey

Saying 'YES' has opened so many doors for me, personally and professionally. Often this has taken me way out of my comfort zone, given me opportunities to meet incredible people, to travel and take unknown paths that on reflection, I was destined to follow.

I often joke with my son, I will be the old girl in retirement home, heels on (even though I can't walk), lipstick applied and I am sure wearing some sparkle. I will be laughing to myself, remembering how one 'YES' changed everything.

'It's never just a facial ® ...'

About Andrea Simpson

Andrea Simpson is an multi award-winning facialist, global educator, best selling author, speaker and solopreneur; and founder of The Facial Mentor, with over two decades of experience blending cutting-edge skin technology with intuitive Ayurvedic wisdom.

Renowned for her signature Autograph Facials and a waitlist of over a year,Andrea has treated celebrities, royalty and high-profile clients alike.Voted Facialist of the Year by BABTAC, she's a trusted voice in advanced skin therapies and holistic aesthetics.

Through her signature education and mentoring, Andrea empowers the next generation of facialists to combine skill with soul. Her approach, anchored in the belief that "It's never just a facial®" has redefined what treatments and skincare can feel like.

With this chapter, she shares the mindset, lesson, life and industry insights that have shaped her journey,offering inspiration and practical guidance to empower the next generation of beauty, wellness leaders and skin lovers alike.

www.andreasimpson.co.uk

www.thefacialmentor.co.uk

Instagram: @andreasimpson_facialist

Instagram: @the_facial_mentor

The Beauty Of The Journey

Serena Morrison

If we were sitting across from each other right now—cups of coffee in hand—I'd tell you that a career in beauty is so much more than perfect nails, flawless brows, or glowing skin. It's a journey. One that has twists and turns, surprises, and lessons. For me, it's been powerful and rewarding.

I've been in this industry for over 40 years, and I can honestly say it's given me more than I could have dreamed of. Not always in the ways I expected—but always in the ways I needed.

Let me take you back—not just to the beginning of my career—but to the very first spark.

I wasn't the girl who spent hours in front of the mirror perfecting her look. Quite the opposite. I was the one out in boots and jeans, hair pulled back, riding ponies all day long. I loved the outdoors and didn't enjoy school much, but I loved learning—especially anything to do with horses.

Beauty wasn't even on my radar. But during a careers meeting, someone suggested beauty therapy because I was physically active and could go on to teach exercise classes. Strange how the right words at the right time can open an entirely new path.

So I enrolled in beauty college. My sister had paved the way a year before me—she's still in the industry today, living in New

Zealand with a successful teaching career behind her and is a former President of the New Zealand Association of Registered Beauty Professionals.

Once qualified, I landed my first job in a salon. I loved it. There was something deeply fulfilling about helping people feel good about themselves. I had a fantastic company product rep who taught me everything she knew and supported me in those early days. Her belief in me encouraged me to learn as much as possible, and my clients benefited from my growing skills.

That passion never left me.

I also had a deep wanderlust, which I credit to my mother, who travelled internationally for work. She was elegant and stylish. Though I didn't share her fashion sense, I admired it. When I heard about working on cruise ships, my curiosity was sparked. I went for it, and those three years aboard were some of the most formative of my life. I was sent off on training courses before leaving for Vancouver, Canada and my very first ship.

I travelled the world, met people from all walks of life, and learned so much—about beauty, yes, but also about resilience, adaptability, and connection. It truly was an adventure.

But eventually, it was time to come home.

I returned and trained to become a teacher, working in a beauty college to gain experience. I enjoyed teaching, but the structure—the same hours, same walls every day – just didn't feel right.

A stint at a Clarins counter reignited my spark. I loved teaching women in small groups, hosting large events, selling products, and offering treatments. I was back to sharing knowledge and helping customers improve their skin health.

But life shifted again, as it does. I moved house and ended up taking over my sister's mobile beauty business when she emigrated to New Zealand. She handed me a thriving business with a healthy client base. It gave me flexibility, control, and the freedom to shape my days. I threw myself into upskilling, learning to run a business, and evolving as both a therapist and an entrepreneur. I loved building relationships with clients just as much as delivering treatments and learned how to plan treatment courses for optimal results.

One day, I came across an ad for a training position in waxing, electrolysis, and ear piercing. It felt like the perfect next step, and I wanted it badly. I remember walking into the interview determined to make it mine – and two days later, I got the call. The job was mine. Over 30 years later, I still work for the same man that gave me that chance. It's a career I love and one that blends beautifully with salon life.

That role had it all: teaching, travelling, visiting salons, and diving into the industry from a whole new perspective. I met hundreds of salon owners – some thriving, some struggling – and each one taught me something. In the back of my mind, a voice began whispering: what would I do differently if this were my salon?

Eventually, the training brought me to Northern Ireland. I fell in love with the landscape, the people – and yes, an Irishman. We married, and before long, a friend told me about a new opportunity: a village salon was for sale. "You have to go," she said. So, I went. I bought it. And 19 years later, I'm still here.

Owning my salon has been one of the most fulfilling chapters of my life. It's not just a business – it's a hub of connection. My clients become friends. We laugh, we cry, we support one another. Every day, my team and I aim to make a difference – whether that's helping someone feel more confident, offering a listening ear, or giving expert skincare advice.

We bring out our clients' inner beauty by enhancing what's on the outside. That's the real magic of this industry.

The opportunities keep coming. I spent a few years dipping in and out of the TV and film industry as a makeup artist. Working here in Northern Ireland and overseas in Croatia and Spain for months at a time, and that experience led to celebrities requesting treatments with me as I was known for being professional and discreet. The beauty industry is full of surprises, and the right attitude will always open new doors.

Then, everything shifted again.

A few years ago, I woke up one Saturday morning knowing something was wrong. I couldn't put my finger on it, I just didn't feel myself. I had wedding makeup booked that day, and, not wanting to let anyone down, I powered through. One of my therapists saw I was struggling and insisted I go home. My husband drove me to the hospital – and by the time we arrived, I'd lost my speech and the use of one side of my body.

I'd had a stroke.

It changed everything in an instant.

But here's the thing, I didn't realise it at the time but that stroke gave me a new lens on life. It reminded me of the "why" behind everything I do: the love I have for my clients, my team, and this beautiful, ever-evolving industry. It grounded me. It refocused me.

It made me more determined than ever to keep doing what I love. Every day I'm still learning, still growing. That's what I love most in this continually evolving world of beauty. It's fascinating. It's exciting. And it gives back in ways you can only dream of.

I've been fortunate to work with some amazing mentors and coaches who've helped me find my voice and shape my business into something I'm proud of. My career has grown with me. It continues to evolve, just as I do. You truly can choose your path again and again to suit your lifestyle, your age, and your interests. That's what I've done, and you can too.

Some Advice From An Oldie

- Whether you're just starting out or have been around the beauty block a few times, remember this:
- Your passion is your superpower. When you genuinely love what you do, your clients feel it—and they'll keep coming back for more than just a treatment.
- Be a lifelong learner. Trends change. Products evolve. Technology advances. Stay curious. Take courses. Ask questions. Invest in your growth.
- Connection is everything. Whether it's a five-minute chat during a brow wax or a deeper conversation, never underestimate the power of human connection.
- Trust your instincts. They led you here for a reason.
- Take care of yourself. We give so much to others—don't forget to look after you.
- There's no one right path. My journey wasn't straightforward. Yours may be different. That's okay. The beauty industry is flexible and full of possibility.

If you're just starting out, know this: you've chosen a career that's rewarding beyond words. You will change lives. You will be changed too.

And if you're an old hand like me? Share your knowledge. Support the next generation.

And never stop learning.

We're not just in the business of beauty – we're in the business of confidence, care, and connection. That's something worth celebrating.

The immeasurable possibilities in the beauty industry are not to be underestimated. The twists and turns can lead you on journeys you've not yet imagined, and who knows, you could be putting it all in a book one day.

About Serena Morrison

With over 43 years of experience as a beauty therapist and 19 years as a dedicated salon owner, Serena Morrison has built a career grounded in passion, expertise, and a genuine love for helping others feel confident in their own skin. She continues to provide hands-on treatments in her busy salon while also holding a long-standing training role with Studex, delivering ear piercing education.

Serena is a firm believer in lifelong learning and regularly updates her skills and qualifications to stay at the forefront of the ever-evolving beauty industry. Her career has taken her on many exciting adventures, and her love of travel remains strong.

Now settled in a peaceful seaside village in Northern Ireland, Serena enjoys the best of both worlds—professional success and a supportive, close-knit, community of friends. Her story is one of resilience, reinvention, and an enduring passion for beauty and wellbeing.

The immeasurable possibilities in the beauty industry are not to be underestimated. The twists and turns can lead you on journeys you've not yet imagined, and who knows, you could be putting it all in a book one day.

Salon website: https://www.sereneskincare.co.uk/

Instagram: https://www.instagram.com/sereneskincarekillyleagh

Facebook: https://www.facebook.com/sereneskincare

Email: info@sereneskincare.co.uk

Nothing Fabulous Happens In Your Comfort Zone

Rebecca Elsdon

I can trace the beginning of my business journey to one bold conversation with my husband. We stood together, staring at the unused space above our garage, and I said, "That's going to be my skin clinic." His face said it all. With three kids under five and no existing client base, it sounded a little... ambitious. He looked at me and said, "How are you going to have the time?"

"I'll find the time," I replied.

And I did.

It started with a few eye rolls and then a hammer in his hand. He got to work, and so did I. That small room above our garage was soon transformed into a beautiful little salon, a space where I could help people feel confident in their skin. It felt perfect. Except for one glaring problem: I had zero clients.

I was still studying for my Level 4 qualification at the time, but I knew I couldn't wait for everything to fall into place. I had to start somewhere. So, I began working on the faces of my family and friends. Anyone who would let me near them with a consultation and a plan, I was game. I chatted with other mums at baby groups and playdates, gently planting the seed about what I did and how I could help.

Back then, I was wearing every possible hat - therapist, receptionist, cleaner, accountant, and, thanks to having no marketing budget, my own social media manager. But the lack of resources forced me to be resourceful. I learned quickly, leaned into digital platforms, and started to see the power of showing up online.

I often joke that for the first two years of building my business, I didn't watch a minute of TV. Every evening, after the chaos of bedtime with three little ones, I'd sit down, open my laptop, and work on the business. There was no glamorous launch, no big marketing spend. Just grit, persistence, and passion.

Three years in, my clinic was growing, slowly but steadily. Because I was based at home and didn't benefit from foot traffic, the growth felt uphill. But I was proud. And then, like a cruel twist of fate, COVID hit.

The world stopped.

My business was still young. I'd poured every spare second and ounce of energy into building it, and now I was told to shut it down. It felt like watching a sandcastle I'd lovingly built get wiped away by a wave.

I had a choice: sink or swim.

And swimming was the only option. I'm not someone who gives up easily, and failure, especially after how far I'd come, was not on the table.

So, I pivoted. I realised something powerful: I had hours available now that I didn't have before. Hours I'd previously spent in the treatment room were suddenly open, and I knew I had to use them wisely. This wasn't the end of my business; this was a rare opportunity to work on it instead of in it.

I created a daily schedule that included homeschooling my kids in the mornings and growing my business in the afternoons and evenings. It was intense, but I was on a mission. I knew that if I wanted my business to survive this, I had to be brave.

There was one thing I had always avoided: showing my face on social media. The idea terrified me. I'd dabbled here and there but kept my content safe, product shots, quotes, client results. But now I had nothing to lose, and I suspected that this one uncomfortable action could be a game-changer.

So I ripped the plaster off.

I announced that I would go live on Instagram the next morning. I had no script, no fancy setup, just me, a quiet room, and a shaky voice. It felt like a disaster. I stumbled over my words, forgot half of what I wanted to say, and spent the rest of the day convinced I looked ridiculous.

But then something unexpected happened: the messages started coming in.

People were thanking me, asking questions, and showing genuine interest. Maybe it hadn't been the car crash I'd imagined. So, I did it again the next day. And then again. And again.

I went live every single morning at 8am for three months straight.

It gave me purpose during a time when so many of us felt lost. It gave me structure and routine. Most importantly, it gave me connection. People from all over the country began booking online consultations, asking for product recommendations, and engaging with my content. Many of them had never met me in person, but they trusted me. I had shown up consistently, shared my knowledge, and let them see the real me.

That period was transformational.

By the time lockdown ended, I had matched my pre-COVID monthly income, without touching a single face. I had doubled the number of clients I was helping with their skin, and for the first time, I had the income to invest in my very first piece of capital equipment.

It was proof of something I'd believed deep down for a long time:

Nothing fabulous happens in your comfort zone.

That quote became my mantra. I repeated it every time I doubted myself, every time I was tempted to shrink back. And it never failed me.

A year later, my home-based clinic had grown to a point where I couldn't manage it alone. I hired my first team members, a therapist and a receptionist, and we started to outgrow the space above the garage. It was time to take another leap.

One day, I spotted a commercial unit for sale. It was in a dream location, surrounded by shops, with lots of passing trade. But it was expensive and needed a full renovation. The old fears crept in. What if it's too much? What if it doesn't work?

But I reminded myself who I had become during lockdown, the woman who showed up every day on Instagram, the woman who refused to sink, the woman who knew how to back herself. I had already proven to myself what could happen when I leaned into discomfort.

So we went for it.

We got the keys a few months later, and the work began. It was chaotic, exciting, terrifying, and exhilarating all at once. But I had a vision. And more than that, I had proof that doing scary things brought incredible rewards.

In our first year in the new premises, we doubled the business. The following year, we did it again.

That little clinic above the garage became the foundation of something extraordinary.

But let me be clear: it wasn't easy. There have been hurdles, many of them. Staff changes, financial stresses, unexpected disruptions. But with each challenge, I've returned to the same principle: push past your comfort zone. If it feels scary, it probably means growth is on the other side.

Looking back now, I realise that some of the most defining moments of my business journey came from decisions I didn't feel ready for. There was no perfect time. No textbook strategy. Just small, consistent actions built on belief and courage.

To anyone starting out or stuck in the middle of the messy building phase, let me say this: you don't need everything to be perfect to begin. You don't need all the answers. But you do need to back yourself. Even when it's hard. Especially when it's hard.

You'll never regret investing in yourself or your dreams. The regret only comes when we stay still, when we choose safety over potential.

I could have waited until the kids were older. I could have waited until I had a bigger budget. I could have waited until I felt "ready" to go live on Instagram.

But I didn't. And that has made all the difference.

Tips I've Learned Along the Way

1. Done is better than perfect.

Perfectionism can be paralysing. If I had waited for the perfect setup, perfect moment, or perfect plan, I'd still be waiting. Start where you are, with what you have, and refine as you go.

2. Your face is your brand.

People buy from people they trust. Showing up on social media felt scary at first, but it was the single most powerful move I made for my business. Your audience wants to know you, your knowledge, your personality, and your passion.

3. Time is never "found," it's created.

Balancing young children and a start-up wasn't easy, but I made time for what mattered. That might mean sacrificing TV or social events, but short-term discipline leads to long-term freedom.

4. The hard times will shape you.

Lockdown could have ended my business, but it ended up redefining it. Challenges force us to be innovative, adaptable, and stronger than we ever imagined. Don't resist the hard seasons, lean into them.

5. Build trust before you sell.

During my closure, I focused on educating my audience, offering value, and showing up consistently. Sales followed naturally because I had already earned their trust. Always give before you ask.

6. Growth rarely feels comfortable.

Whether it's going live for the first time, hiring your first staff member, or moving into bigger premises, growth usually comes wrapped in fear. That's how you know it's the right move.

7. Have a vision but be flexible.

I never imagined how my business would evolve, but I stayed open to new opportunities. Keep your long-term vision in mind, but don't be afraid to pivot when circumstances change.

8. Celebrate the small wins.

From your first online booking to your first client review, acknowledge every milestone. These moments are the stepping stones to the big goals.

9. Invest before you feel ready.

Whether it's equipment, staff, or training, growth often requires a leap of faith. If the numbers make sense and the passion is there, bet on yourself.

10. Nothing fabulous happens in your comfort zone.

This is the mantra that has guided every bold move I've made. Discomfort is where the magic happens. When you feel fear, you're often on the edge of something brilliant.

About Rebecca Elsdon

With 20 years in the beauty industry, Rebecca has gained a wealth of knowledge and a reputation as a highly regarded facialist and skin expert. Her approach to treating the skin is both scientific and holistic to improve skin health and achieve results. Steering away from the skincare 'fads' she delivers results-driven, clinic treatment and ensures her clients get the support they need on their journey to healthier skin. Successfully treating acne, rosacea, and pigmentation, Rebecca thrives off challenging skin conditions, stating "when people begin to feel confident in their skin, lives change." Rebecca now leads a team of skin therapists in her high-end clinic focused on giving their best to their clients and helping them regain their confidence. Her commitment to her clients and therapists is clear to see from the ongoing success of her growing clinic.

Website: www.reskinclinic.co.uk

Instagram: https://www.instagram.com/rebeccaelsdonadvancedskin/?hl=en

Instagram clinic page: https://www.instagram.com/reskinclinic_/?hl=en

LinkedIn: https://www.linkedin.com/in/rebecca-elsdon-8599b9146/

Email: rebecca@reskinclinic.co.uk

Beauty, Business And Baby Owls

Fiona Jackson

It feels surreal to say I've worked in this industry for 24 years. When I look back, I don't see years – I see moments, memories, people, laughter, tears (clients and my own), the smell of freshly painted nails (that apparently smell like "baby owls," according to one client!) and countless experiences that have brought me to where I am today.

The beauty industry isn't just about nails and waxing (that was my brother's take on it when I chose it as my career path) - it's about people, connections and the incredible power of human touch. I am in awe of the Beauty Industry: of what it can achieve, of what it has allowed me to achieve and if you are just stepping into it ....what the endless possibilities are within it!

Life Choices

At school, I had a decision to make: do I go to university and become a teacher, or do I follow a more hands on, creative path? If I'm honest, the realisation that I didn't have 4 years at university in me is what led me to beauty therapy. Having made my decision, I never looked back. My college years spent at Glasgow College of Commerce were shaped by a single, ambitious plan: to work on luxury cruise ships, travel the world and, one day, have a business of my own.

Life at Sea

Towards the end of my second year at college my dream became a reality when I secured a job with Steiner! After training in Watford, I boarded the MS Norwegian Sun (which was home for nearly a year), as an Elemis therapist. Life onboard in the spa was glamorous, challenging, exhausting and exhilarating all at once – if there was an award for burning the candle at both ends, I'd have it!

I will never forget being at sea on 9/11. The world felt terrifyingly uncertain. I was frightened, so were my clients. Passengers and crew turned to us not just for facials or massages, but for comfort and human connection. It was then I truly realised the emotional depth of my chosen career. We might be called beauty therapists, but so often we're therapists in the truest sense - quiet listeners, providing a safe space and a comforting voice.

The understanding I gained during this time has singlehandedly shaped the way I've approached so many things in the industry. A simple brow shape or manicure isn't "just" that; it's a moment where someone should feel valued and cared for.

From Sea To Salon

Returning to dry land (sleeping through an entire transatlantic flight – asleep before take-off and had to be woken for landing…..that's my candle burning at both ends), my next dream was on the horizon: my own salon. With savings from my time at sea, I opened Diva having been given a rare opportunity by my then employer, Alison. She wanted to change direction and concentrate solely on face and body treatments and offered me the remaining client base – this was my start, and I grabbed it with both hands. In the early days, it was just me, a logo I designed myself (after agonising over fonts and colours – there were no Apps to do it back in the day!), and a small group of loyal clients.

Building Diva wasn't easy. At the age of 22 I was naive with a LOT to learn (I'm still learning today). I did learn quickly that passion isn't enough - you also need spreadsheets (not my favourite), systems in place and sleep (when you can get your brain to switch off!). Thankfully, my brother helped me set up a very simple accounting system (he knew my maths abilities were basic), which kept me on the right track financially. Within the first year, I bought my first home, which is a milestone that still makes me proud.

Over the years, Diva has grown, won awards and evolved. We've been in three premises, each move reflecting not just expansion but vision: adding more treatment rooms, more therapists and new services. It wasn't just about getting bigger - it was about creating a space that felt special, welcoming and professional, where our clients felt part of something. Today, being in the salon and hearing laughter and conversation in every room reminds me how far we've come from those very early days.

Moments And Memories

Some of my favourite moments have little to do with the treatments themselves. Like the client who gave me a mug saying, "I'm a beautician, not a magician," or Jackie, who told me she loves when her nails are first done as they smell like "baby owls."

(I still don't know what that really means, or what a baby owl even smells like, but it's still one of my favourite client stories!).

Clients open up during treatments in a way they might not anywhere else. Over the years, I've shared tears over bereavements, celebrated engagements and pregnancies, and offered support through divorce and illness – some of life's toughest challenges. These emotional connections are the heartbeat of what we do.

At Diva, I've always encouraged my team (who are a hugely important part of the business) to bring their individuality to treatments. It's not about ticking boxes; it's about creating an experience. Some of my clients have been with me since the very beginning, nearly 22 years ago. That loyalty isn't built overnight, it's built on trust, consistency and genuine care.

Stepping Into Educating

Remember that career decision I had - teaching or beauty? In the end, I found a way to do both.

During my time at sea, I was promoted to onboard Elemis trainer and discovered how much I loved sharing knowledge. Back home, I completed my teacher training (PTLLS) and have spent 17 years teaching across three different colleges, enjoying the privilege of working with the next generation of therapists.

This love for teaching has evolved into creating RISE, a programme I'm currently designing to mentor new therapists and help bridge the gap between education and the realities of industry. Because the truth is: college teaches skills, but it doesn't always prepare you for the retailing, rebooking, or the emotional intelligence needed to handle real clients.

My goal with RISE is to help therapists feel excited, confident and ready to start their careers. It's about giving them the tools, mindset and the belief that they can do this - and do it successfully.

Staying Inspired

One of the rather unexpected gifts of my career has been the chance to combine my love of travel with business and personal growth.

Over the years, I've attended multiple Professional Beauty events across the UK, visited Cosmoprof in Las Vegas several times and in the last 12 months, have made time to join business retreats in Manchester and Malta.

These experiences have allowed me to step away from my day-to-day life to reflect, learn, build my network and return with fresh ideas for Diva and for myself. They're more than trips; they are an essential part of staying inspired (there's always something new in this industry), evolving (both personally and in business) and reminding myself why I love what I do.

Wearing Many Hats (And Learning it's Ok to Take Some Off!)

Running a salon means being a therapist, manager, HR, marketing team, bookkeeper, cleaner, handyman and counsellor all at once (and sometimes all in one day!). Nobody warns you about this when you start (or they certainly didn't tell me). We are not taught how to run a business; you learn by doing, by making mistakes, and by picking yourself back up again.

In the early years, I tried to do everything myself.

Spoiler: it doesn't work! Burnout taught me that we can't be good at everything and the importance of asking for help and delegating.

One of the biggest pieces in my entrepreneurial puzzle is support. I am quite sure I am one of very few women who can say that I've proudly worked with my mother-in-law for 19 years..... and only fallen out twice! Then there's my husband Dave. He's been there from the very start, cheering me on quietly behind the scenes. Over the last ten years especially, he's become my essential business partner – and now company Director. Clients might not see him, but his support, knowledge and weird (but very handy) love of spreadsheets has been invaluable. From keeping the finances organised to encouraging me to introduce new systems (I'm a bit of a technophobe), his calm perspective (and ability to keep me calm) has often helped me see a way forward. Diva would not be what it is today without Dave and Kath, and I'm forever grateful.

It's A Community, Not Just AClient List

One of my proudest achievements isn't on a balance sheet, it's the community we've built at Diva. Clients call it their "Diva family," and it truly feels that way. It's a place where people feel safe to be themselves, share their worries, fears, joy, sadness and happiness and can leave feeling a little lighter – this is true for both staff and clients.

This sense of community extends beyond clients, too. In my early days, I had a network of local, supportive female business owners who offered advice, shared contacts and listened when I needed to vent. I've always tried to pay that forward by encouraging collaboration over competition. There's room for everyone, and we rise by lifting others.

Challenges And Bumps In The Road

Nobody said being a business owner is easy because, if it were, everyone would do it! There have been tough times: economic downturns, the pandemic, staff changes and simply the everyday worries that come with running a business.

But every challenge has taught me something: how to adapt, how to communicate better, how to keep going even when it feels impossible. The key isn't to avoid failure - it's learning from it and to keep moving forward.

What I've Learned (So Far!)

- **Client relationships are key** - Trust and consistency build loyalty that can last decades.
- **Emotional intelligence is just as important as technical skill** - A perfect set of nails means little if your client doesn't feel heard and valued.
- **Mentorship matters** - We all need people who believe in us, challenge us and guide us.
- **Keep learning** - The industry changes constantly; so be curious as it will keep you relevant.
- **Don't be shy: ask for help.** You can't (and shouldn't!) do everything alone.
- **Choose your staff wisely** - Encourage, care for and respect them.
- **Celebrate your wins** - Even the small ones.
- **Multitasking** - Some days you're a therapist. Other days, a therapist, life coach, travel agent, unofficial wedding planner……. sometimes all in one appointment!
- **Prepare for anything** - No amount of training prepares you for a client who says their nails smell like "baby owls" – every day is different in this industry!

- **Spreadsheets** - They might not be glamorous, but knowing your numbers will help keep you in business.
- **Burnout** - It's avoidable so ensure self-care is part of your plan.
- **Social media** - It can be a powerful tool but remember that real connection still happens face to face.
- **Don't be frightened of change** – Your business will evolve, and so will you. Learn to embrace it.

An Industry I Adore

This industry has given me so much: the chance to travel the world, to be a therapist, trainer, educator, mentor, business owner, speaker and author. It's brought me friendships, laughter, purpose - and yes, even mugs and baby owl stories.

I feel genuinely lucky to do work that I love, in an industry that's about so much more than what's on the surface. We change how people feel, not just how they look and that's an incredibly privileged position to hold.

To anyone starting out: be prepared to embrace every opportunity. Be ready to work hard but remember why you started. Keep learning, keep connecting and above all, never underestimate the power of kindness and human touch.

And to my fellow business owners: delegate, breathe, and remember - you're making magic, even if your mug says otherwise!

About Fiona Jackson

As the proud founder of Diva, Fiona has spent over 22 years building not just a salon, but a place clients fondly call their "Diva family."

Known as a multitasker and a social butterfly, she's rarely happier than when sharing a bowl of pasta and a glass of red with friends. Fiona's approach to life (and business) is simple: say "yes" to the challenge first and figure out the how later!

Beyond running the salon and developing her mentorship programme RISE, you'll often find her braving the open water for a swim (yes, even in Scotland!), enduring zero degree ice training, (she hates the cold but loves the power it has for both mind and body) or simply planning her next challenge.

Fiona's journey is fuelled by her love of people, connection and good conversation - all balanced by the support and patience of her husband Dave, and plenty of cuddles from her completely spoiled Cavapoo, Riley.

www.instagram.com/fionajacksonmentor

www.linkedin.com/in/fiona-jackson-diva

www.fionajackson.net

hello@fionajackson.net

www.divalanark.co.uk

The Little Salon That Could

Gemma Holt

You know that moment when you're about to leave school and you have no idea if you're making the right decision? You wonder if the path you're choosing is going to lead somewhere brilliant; or if you'll look back one day and think, "What on earth was I doing?"

Well, 26 years on, I can safely say... I absolutely did make the right choice.

My career started when I was 15. I sat my last exam on a Friday, and by the following Monday, I was starting my apprenticeship in a salon. I was incredibly lucky to be offered the opportunity as the salon only employed an apprentice every two years, and all training was done on-site because the salon owner was qualified to teach. I didn't know it at the time, but being taught by this amazing lady was going to shape me in ways I could never have imagined. Her attention to detail was phenomenal - every single treatment had to be perfect and that kind of training stays with you forever. She not only made me the therapist I am today, but she also became one of my lifelong friends. Sara Shoemark, I can never thank you enough for what you did for me.

I qualified with Sara and stayed at her salon for five years, until one of my clients asked me a question that would change everything: would I be interested in joining a brand-new spa opening in Chester?

It wasn't just any spa – it was The Chester Grosvenor. A five-star hotel, owned by the Duke and Duchess of Westminster, in the heart of Chester city centre. As soon as I heard that, something lit up in me. Not only was it an incredible opportunity, but it also felt personal as my Dad had worked for the Duke as a herdsman, and we'd lived on the Duke's Estate for most of my childhood.

And it really was amazing. I was involved in everything from the spa design, to selecting products and choosing uniforms. It wasn't just a job; it felt like building something from the ground up. I started as a therapist but worked my way up to Assistant Manager within three years.

But then... tragedy struck and I had to give it all up. It was beyond my control and heartbreaking. When I was 18, my knee started to dislocate. At first, it was just every now and again, but over the next five years, it became a recurring nightmare. It reached a point where my doctors told me I had to give up my career and move to a desk job.

So, at 23, I had to start all over again.

The next eight years were spent in a world I never imagined myself in: offices, spreadsheets, accountancy, PA work. I was good at it, and I made it work but it wasn't me. I missed the creativity, the energy, the connection with people and, eventually, realised that I wanted to go back to being a therapist.

In June 2014, I took the plunge and opened Lily's Beauty Salon in my hometown of Whitchurch – the salon had five treatment rooms, three nail stations and a large relaxation lounge. I started with three therapists and we hit the ground running. The salon gained in reputation and size until eventually I expanded to having a team of seven. The salon carried on at this size with full diaries, long opening hours and all the chaos and benefits that go along with a large salon. In 2017, two life-changing events happened in the same year: I had my little boy, Charlie, and then a few months later, my Dad suddenly fell ill and passed away.

I was on maternity leave, juggling all the highs and lows that come with having a new baby, grieving for Dad and trying to help Mum sell her property and downsize, when a member of staff left and I immediately had to return to work.

I was completely overwhelmed and exhausted. I didn't know if I had the strength to carry on and seriously considered selling the business as I couldn't see a way forward. Eventually, the dust settled, and I had time to re-evaluate and concluded that downsizing would alleviate some of the pressure.

We found a Grade II listed character property on the high street and set about renovating it over the course of two months, whilst still juggling the other salon, finally opening in November 2020 with three treatment rooms, two nail desks and a small waiting area.

I can honestly say that I did not struggle with the idea of reducing the size of the salon – that bigger isn't necessarily better. Some may have seen it as a failure but it was a huge relief to me. I focused on our existing clients and making their experience the best it could be; with an intimate, luxury space where they felt even more nurtured and cared for than before.

And do you know what happened?

The business became more profitable than ever.

Why? We went back to basics; focusing on the client experience and finer detail such as fresh plants, as well as more traditional flowers, which are more sustainable and also have meaning and help oxygenate the environment.

I gave the therapists more time with clients which gives them the opportunity not only to have more connection but also to discuss new treatments and products – an extra fifteen minutes can really elevate the bottom line.

I wanted Lily's to feel like a retreat from the daily stresses of life. A pause button. A moment of "me time" where clients can breathe and feel looked after. That's why our clients keep coming back. That's why they are happy to wait for appointments or drive 40 minutes for a facial or a massage. Once you've experienced a space where you feel genuinely cared for, not just processed, it's hard to settle for anything less. We know our clients – their families, their lives, the triumphs and the sadnesses.

With this monumental shift in the salon came the awards. I had entered the Professional Beauty awards previously and been shortlisted six times but had never won. In 2021, Lily's won Professional Beauty Salon of the Year. In 2022, 2023 and 2024, we won BABTAC & CIBTAC Small Salon of the Year, culminating in receiving the Platinum Status award for winning over three consecutive years.

People often ask me how we've managed to win so many awards. I believe it's because we've stayed focused. We know who we are. We're not trying to be everything to everyone. Lily's is about high standards, warm service, and a personal touch that clients can feel. It's not flashy. It's thoughtful. It's consistent. And it works.

In 2024, Lily's had its ten year anniversary. I think it's important to celebrate these milestones, not only for you but for the staff and clients.

More recently, I have been invited to speak at industry events and sit on judging panels, which I enjoy immensely and hope to do more of in the future. I love that I have a story to tell and might be able to help others find their way and what works for them.

All I can say is that, ultimately, small really has worked for me.

When you stop trying to please everyone, you start pleasing the right people - the clients who get it. The clients who come back. The ones who tell their friends, leave glowing reviews, and genuinely feel part of your story. That's priceless.

I know this might sound silly after ten years, but every time a client says something like, "It's just so lovely here," or "I've never had a facial like that before," it still gives me butterflies. Because that's what Lily's is about. We're not trying to be a franchise. We're not trying to take over the world. We're just trying to do our bit beautifully - in our own little corner of Shropshire.

So if you're reading this and thinking, "Should I scale back?" or "What if I stopped chasing the bigger, louder, busier version of success?" Let me tell you something:

You absolutely can, and it can be better than you ever imagined.

Quieter, yes. Simpler, maybe. But more profitable, more joyful, and a thousand times more sustainable.

At Lily's, we do fewer treatments a day but we do them brilliantly.

We don't have a huge team but we have a strong one.

We may not be the biggest but we're one of the best.

And that's more than enough for me.

About Gemma Holt

Gemma has spent over 26 years in the beauty industry. She is the founder and owner of Lily's Beauty Salon, a multi award-winning boutique salon, established in 2014. Under her leadership, the salon has won numerous accolades, including Professional Beauty Boutique Salon of the Year 2021, BABTAC Small Salon of the Year in both 2022 and 2023, and a BABTAC Platinum Status recognition award.

Gemma regularly appears as a guest speaker at shows and serves as a judge on the panel for Professional Beauty.

Looking to the future, Gemma is passionate about helping and inspiring the next generation of beauty professionals and salon owners. She is especially keen on encouraging others to discover their salon's unique identity and find their USP.

When she's not running her business, Gemma loves spending time with her husband and son. They are very much part of their local community, often found enjoying their allotment or a game of crown green bowls.

www.lilysbeautysalon.co.uk

info@lilysbeautysalon.co.uk

www.instagram.com/lilyswhitchurch

www.facebook.com/lilysbeautysalonwhitchurch

A New Chapter

Zoe Threadgold

If you'd told me at the start of my career that this is where I'd end up, I wouldn't have believed you.

As a skin therapist, I've always been on the lookout for that next exciting product or treatment – something truly different. I consider myself incredibly fortunate to have found NeurotriS. It came into my life at just the right moment, and it changed everything.

The Foundations

My journey in the beauty industry began back in 1985 when I qualified as a beauty therapist. Fresh out of training, I landed a job in a local salon and couldn't wait to get started. Five years later, at the age of 22, I took over the business. At the time, it didn't feel like a big decision – it just felt right.

But as time went on and my family came along, I realised how hard it was to juggle running a busy salon with being a mum. I often felt like I wasn't giving either role the attention it deserved.

That's when I made the decision to create a home salon and work my hours around my family – which I did for the next

15 years. It gave me the flexibility I needed. More recently, I returned to clinic life, working three days a week and renting space. It was a balance that worked – until the world turned upside down.

When The World Stopped

Lockdown was, without doubt, one of the strangest times of my career. A strange time for all of us. It was both unsettling and oddly illuminating. One minute we were working as normal, the next we were told to stop. Just like that, everything changed. Something that had always been such a huge part of my identity was suddenly taken away, and it left me feeling completely unanchored.

There was shock, of course, but then came the wave, sadness, frustration, fear, and a very real sense of uncertainty. I honestly thought that might be it – the end of the road for me as a therapist. After so many years doing what I loved, I found myself wondering what came next.

But like so many others in our industry, I didn't stay down for long. We're a resilient, resourceful bunch. I dug deep and started to explore – signing up for courses, learning new things, keeping my mind busy. It was a time of reflection, but also rediscovery. I gave myself the space to think about what I really wanted from the next chapter of my career.

And it was during that time, quite unexpectedly, that I came across NeurotriS.

A Lockdown Discovery

During those endless days of lockdown, I started using a home microcurrent device from the US called the PicoToner by NeurotriS. I wasn't expecting anything groundbreaking – but what I saw surprised me. The results were visible, and I actually enjoyed using it.

Once I was back in the clinic, I found myself thinking, "If the home device is this good, what are the professional systems like?" That curiosity quickly turned into something much more.

A Leap Of Faith To California

As there was no UK distributor, I decided to take a leap and flew to California to visit the company and see the devices for myself. While I was there, I met Tony, the CEO of NeurotriS. During one of our conversations, he casually mentioned they didn't have a distributor in the UK and asked if I might be interested.

I laughed and said, "Absolutely not!" I hadn't even remotely considered the idea.

But then I brought a device back home and started using it in clinic. The results were undeniable. My clients were seeing transformations we hadn't been able to achieve before.

I've always believed in working with the body, not against it – supporting the skin and muscles in the way they were naturally designed to function. NeurotriS technology aligned completely with that philosophy.

I realised quite quickly that this technology wasn't just good – it was special. I also began to see a business opportunity that could offer therapists access to it here in the UK.

My husband Rob has a design and marketing background and runs his own business, so his skillset sits perfectly alongside mine to make this venture possible. We genuinely believed in the technology and the capabilities of the systems. But starting this business was also going to be a big financial leap – so we had to take a step back and think carefully.

After much consideration, I got back in touch with Tony and said, "Can we revisit that conversation about distribution?"

A Business Takes Root

And here we are. Today, we are the UK distributor of a product I truly believe in.

A year ago, we officially launched NeurotriS UK at Professional Beauty Manchester in September 2024. It's been an incredible journey – full of long hours and hard work behind the scenes. But we've always understood that nothing worthwhile comes without effort, and that mindset has kept us focused and motivated throughout.

One of the most rewarding parts has been visiting salons and clinics across the country – meeting solo therapists, teams, and business owners who all share a genuine passion for delivering the very best for their clients. Yes, we're all running businesses, but it's the passion that shines through time and again.

Having spent so many years working alone, it's been truly uplifting to see how each salon brings something unique to the table. It's a privilege to support them – not just with the technology, but in watching them grow and thrive.

New Skills, New Goals

Another hurdle came when I began exploring the idea of having a training course endorsed by Habia. What I hadn't realised at the time was that I would also need an official teaching qualification. So, I enrolled on a teacher training course with Habia to gain the qualification required. This was an intense short course – and not without the tears, long evenings, wine, and chocolate!

I'm now in the process of developing my own training course – a completely new and exciting step for me.

From the beginning, I knew that customer support had to be at the heart of what we do. When someone invests in a system like this, they deserve ongoing support – not just a sales pitch.

But more than that, I've learnt the importance of staying true to your values. Integrity has always mattered to me. It's easy to get caught up in the noise, but I've always believed that if you do things with honesty, care, and consistency, it shows. Whether it's how I treat my clients, communicate with other therapists, or represent a brand – it has to come from a place of genuine belief and ethical practice.

Navigating New Dynamics

Now, I won't pretend setting up a distributorship has been easy. There have been plenty of challenges – not least the fact that Rob and I are now working together for the first time! We trust and respect each other completely in terms of skills and knowledge, but navigating new roles, learning on the job, and adjusting to working side by side has been a learning curve.

It's easy to slip into talking shop 24/7, so we've had to set clear boundaries and make time to switch off.

Social media has been a particularly tricky area for me. If I'm honest – and I always try to be – I find it uncomfortable. I understand its power and the need for brand visibility, but the idea of putting myself "out there" just doesn't sit naturally. It's not just about showcasing a product; it's about showing parts of yourself too. And that's not easy – especially when you've built your career on one-to-one relationships and quiet professionalism.

But I'm learning, adapting, and trying to stay true to myself at the same time.

Looking Back, Looking Forward

Without doubt, the hardest thing I've had to do is step back from the treatment room. It makes me emotional to even write this, because it's been such a huge part of my life for so many years – a space where I've built relationships, grown as a therapist, and found so much joy in helping others.

Over the past year, I've done my best to juggle both worlds – continuing hands-on treatments while building the business – but I've come to realise that for NeurotriS UK to grow in the way I truly believe it can, it needs more of my time, energy, and focus. Most importantly, it needs me to be fully present in offering the level of support I've committed to for those who have invested in the brand.

So now, the time has come for me to give my all to this next chapter. It's a difficult step, but one filled with purpose – and I know in my heart it's the right move forward.

If there's one thing this journey has taught me, it's that we're far more capable than we think – especially when we're passionate about something.

We're allowed to change direction. In fact, sometimes we need to. Our industry is ever-evolving, and so are we.

If I could share one message with anyone reading this – whether you're just starting out or decades into your journey – it would be this:

Work hard. Stay focused. Lead with passion. And above all, believe in what you do.

About Zoe Threadgold

Zoe Threadgold is an experienced skin therapist with a career spanning nearly four decades. Beginning in 1985, she built her own successful salon business before adapting her work to suit family life. During the pandemic, Zoe discovered NeurotriS – an advanced microcurrent technology from the US – which aligned perfectly with her skin philosophy of working with the body, not against it. Inspired by the results and confident in the technology, Zoe and her husband Rob, who has a background in design and marketing, launched NeurotriS UK in 2024. Despite the challenges of starting a distributorship from scratch, Zoe's passion, integrity, and commitment to quality have helped her connect with salons across the UK, sharing a technology she truly believes in. Now also developing a Habia-endorsed training course, Zoe remains focused on supporting therapists and advancing the industry in a genuine, ethical way.

zoe@neurotris.uk

https://www.instagram.com/neurotrisuk

@neurotrisuk

https://www.linkedin.com/in/zoe-threadgold-78137b199/

Do What Lights You Up!

Cindy Woodward

Beauty was never on my radar.

I was a tomboy, no makeup, very sporty and captain of all the teams, but also academic. After A 'Levels I studied Law, and went straight into working in criminal law, fighting the good fight.

In 1992 my Mum opened a toning studio and as any child of self-employed parents knows, you were expected to help in family businesses, and so after a full day at work I'd come home and work in the studio from 6pm-10pm and Saturdays.

I soon realised being around these women who wanted to look after themselves was far more fun than working with people who had broken the law!

Remember, this this was 1992, and the general consensus back then was you only studied beauty if you "weren't academic." So, I sneaked off to the college in the next city and studied after work twice a week for three years. Once qualified, I slowly built my client base up on my day off.

In 1995, Mum bought a CACI machine, we were one of the first salons to get it, the training was rigorous and if you didn't pass, you couldn't have one - be great if it was like that these days. I remember thinking crikey I'll never need this treatment - the naivety of youth!!

Huge curveball in 1999 when my Dad bought his business partner out and, yet again I was called upon to help out. My business had to fit in around Dad's (his was much bigger)

I would work two days for Dad and the rest in mine and this went on for 20 years, the saying "Man plans, God Laughs" springs to mind, but it gave me a huge insight into the stress of running a much bigger business, overheads, staff, VAT etc,

The Bit That's Not Biz Related *

In 1998 I had my first child. I had a week off work (yes, that is illegal) and I remember fibbing to the midwife about working. Olivia was born in November and Christmas was super busy then so I couldn't miss out on that period of business.

We worked childcare between us until she could go into nursery for two days a week at three months old.

I'm often asked by new Mums if I felt bad her going so young, and the answer is absolutely not. I had a business to run, it wasn't an option and I knew that beforehand, plus I knew following my passion would make me a better parent to be around and I could provide more for her future.

Charlie followed in 2002 (three days off work this time round) and was super chilled, so he came to work with me for ten months before going into nursery two days.

My advice to new Mums is just do what feels right for you, don't get hung up on other people's opinions, especially the ones who hate their job or aren't self -employed. The fact is once you are a parent, you generally spend your entire life feeling guilty about something or other anyway.

I'm a believer in "you get out what you put in" and that goes for everything, even parenthood. As a parent, I really tried to be fully present and focused on quality time with the kids when I was with them, and felt that's a whole lot better than being with them more hours and sitting them infront of a screen.

The kids are now 26 and 23 and turned out just fine. Do what works best for you and your personal situation, someone will always have an opinion regardless.

*Now Back To Business

In 2007, Mom was diagnosed with Non-Hodgkin's Lymphoma which was an absolute bolt from the blue. We were due to fly out to their holiday home in Florida for three weeks on the Saturday and she got the diagnosis Friday, so my parents didn't go but we did.

This opened up another world for me. I spent hours in book stores, speaking with alternative therapists, I spent $400 on Biotin, Shark Cartledge, mushroom supplements etc, and came back terrified I'd get stopped for drug trafficking! Weirdly, I also bought the book "The Secret" -perhaps another sign of being way ahead of my time.

Around this time my skin took a major nosedive, with horrific breakouts and my then five year asked "why is your face so spotty Mummy?" and this is what I did for a living – but nothing I did helped.

One Florida visit, a magazine was thrown on the garden called "Natural Awakenings" a free magazine launched by the Universe onto our grass which changed the whole trajectory of my business forever.

There was a salon in the magazine called "Bloom Organics" and I decided to go for a facial.

I walked in and the salon was very Eco, beautiful, tranquil and spa like.

I had an amazing facial using Eminence Organics (which I'd never heard of) and my skin quickly improved, so three times a year when I visited Sarasota, I would book a facial.

I desperately wanted to carry Eminence, but it wasn't yet available in the UK. In hindsight I always wonder if I should have looked at being the distributor, but I had enough on my plate at that time.

My ultimate vision was to create a space where self-care is celebrated, for clients to escape and emerge not only looking radiant, but feeling utterly restored. So, in 2012, with Eminence now available in the UK, I made the bold move of streamlining my treatments purely to the ones I was passionate about.

I researched treatments and products and started carrying product ranges that were organic or as chemical-free as possible whilst still offering amazing results and layering them with technology such as microcurrent and oxygen which was a bit out there in 2012.

I created an entire menu of my own bespoke treatment and protocols in a luxurious and tranquil environment. By combining these with my personal holistic approach to not only beauty and the physical benefits that brings, but also the positive mental benefits, I feel I now have a business which offers way more than "just beauty"

Creating my own treatment protocols has always been a non-negotiable. One of my proudest moments recently was being called "defiant" by a rep because I didn't want to follow their practices, I like to think of it not as defiant, more as "pioneering" I mean, who wants to be like everyone else!

In May 2013, after leading a healthy and vibrant life since her treatment in 2007, my beautiful Mom was diagnosed with terminal Ovarian Cancer, and heartbreakingly lost her battle in July 2014, she was 64 and as youthful and glamourous as ever.

My entire experience and journey with her through her illness set me on the path to where I am today and I'm so glad she saw me begin my real journey in 2012 which I now realise truly is to help others and share my knowledge.

My Middlewood Day Spa is her old toning studio so I know she's here keeping me in check every single day.

In 2017, year I made a significant investment (the sick feeling amount you have to phone your Dad to check you're doing the right thing type) to a business coaching course.

I was allocated a holistic mindset coach and after working with her for a while had the lightbulb moment realising, I wasn't just performing amazing skin treatments. I was naturally coaching my clients without even realising it, sorting their skin and their lives out at the same time without even noticing.

I really started to invest a lot of time working on my own mindset and realising my own potential, which transferred to my clients, and I went onto qualify as a Holistic Mindset Coach. I still work with the same mindset coach now; she calls me out on my faulty thinking or oversights and stops me getting in my own way, which we all need.

Through my knowledge and experiences over the past 11 years I have created a toolbox that I open up, delve into and share with my clients when they need more than help with purely their skin.

I've seen clients really make huge changes in their lives, helping them start their own business, follow a new career path, write a book, travel abroad alone or leave toxic relationships and I love it!

In 2020, I held my first three-day" Give Back To Self-Retreat" combining mindset coaching with skincare and wellness in beautiful surroundings. It was a huge success which we've gone onto repeat since and carry out condensed day versions.

Then Lockdown came!!!

I responded by creating weekly group online facials, held the whole way through, as well as online retreats. My clients loved it, describing it as their lifeline to normality each week. They came out of lockdown with amazing skin and were mini skin gurus after our sessions, and I managed to somehow keep my turnover the same as pre-lockdown.

Roll on 2022, when I hit the VAT threshold - squeaky bum time – I couldn't work any more hours, my prices were significantly higher than anyone else, so the Universe delivered a solution again.

I got an email from a 'businesses for sale' company, and for some random reason opened it.

There was a retirement sale of a salon five miles from me, and although it gave no info, I could work out who it was. It was a lady who had a salon for 45 years and she was retiring.

I called her, asked if it was hers and she said Yes. A week later I bought it, and she gave me one condition that I would keep her therapist of 20 years on as staff.

I was still treating my clients full time, but I wanted to duplicate the whole ethos of the Middlewood salon, so we ripped everything out, floors, ceilings, shopfront over a period of four months and only closed for a week. We went up after the salon closed and my amazing husband would work through the night, fuelled by a pint and bag of crisps..........., the girls would come in the next day thinking the refurb fairies had been in whilst they slept!

I'm two years into having the second salon, and I'm often asked, "Do you regret it?"

I always said, the second salon would either work, or be an expensive lesson.

I don't see anything as a failure, I look for what the lesson is.

Is it stressful? Hell yes!!

Is it worth it? Financially... that's yet to be seen and if I performed treatments for the hours I put into admin, staff training, etc I would be way better off financially. But for me personally I'd say absolutely yes, it's been worth it, at least I won't be sat here in ten years wondering "what if I'd have just......"

I'm 53 now, and the amazing ripple effect is many of my clients look at me grabbing the world by the balls, taking risks and following my passion and think "Well, perhaps I'm not too old, it's not too late, and what's the worst that can happen" which I think makes it all worthwhile.

About Cindy Woodward

Cindy Woodward is the founder of The Beauty Retreat Organic Day Spa.

With over 30 years in the beauty industry, Cindy has a loyal following and reputation for excellence. Her bespoke facial techniques combined with a holistic twist and a sprinkle of mindset, empower you to love the skin you're in.

Cindy is also a certified Holistic Mindset Coach, and mentors others to fulfil their true potential and help them get out of their own way. She holds weekend and day retreats combining mindset, wellness and skincare.

Salon Website: www.thebeautyretreatsheffield.co.uk

LinkedIn: linkedin.com/in/cindy-woodward-754a44a2

Instagram: @beautyretreatsheffield

@cindywoodwardcoaching

Facebook: TheBeautyRetreatSheffield

Email: Info@thebeautyretreatsheffield.co.uk

Growing In Belief

Anna Inglis

I grew up in the seaside town of Torquay with my hard-working parents and two older sisters, who were more academically inclined than me. They were the kind who thrived on structure, exams and ticking the right boxes. I, on the other hand, was far more interested in people.

School never truly captured my attention. I was easily distracted and always drawn to conversations. I had a soft spot for anyone sitting on their own, and always made sure they knew they had a friend in me.

Everything shifted in my teenage years when we moved to the Midlands after my parents separated. Leaving behind friends and familiarity was tough, but it also provided new opportunities. In a new school and new life, something finally sparked my interest.

My new school offered day release NVQ courses, including a basic introduction to beauty therapy.

Suddenly, it all made sense. I remembered giving facials to my grandad as a child, completely absorbed in the experience. The same feeling returned, and I knew there and then, this was my path.

As soon as school ended, I enrolled in an NVQ Beauty Therapy course at college. I juggled studies alongside several part-time jobs: working on an Estée Lauder counter, helping out at a local pub, and reception work at a tanning shop. I thrived on being busy!

My confidence began to grow. I achieved recognition at college for my dedication and application to the course. This was all new to me, and I loved it. The girl who once struggled finally had the fire in her belly, determined to prove to herself she could do it.

As soon as I qualified, I couldn't wait to get started. I walked straight into a job at a local beauty salon, ready to learn, grow, and prove myself all over again.

I spent a brilliant three years in the salon, learning the ropes and building a loyal base of clients. I absolutely loved the day-to-day interaction, and the trust that developed between the clients and I.

But I wanted more! I enrolled in teacher training alongside salon work. Looking back, it's a decision that's been invaluable in building and developing a team.

The salon environment felt so natural, but beneath the surface I was battling with myself. I wanted to be the best, but maybe too much so. The pressure I put myself under drove me forward, but it also seeded doubt.

In the Summer of 2013, sat on a sun lounger on holiday, something clicked. I'm going to do this for myself.

This particular trip was the beginning of a pattern I've come to recognise in myself. Holidays have become the space where I breathe, reflect, and make the big decisions. Even now, as I write this chapter while taking a moment on a family holiday, I realise those moments have led to progress.

Soon enough, I came across Mercia Marina in Willington, the largest in-land marina in Europe. They were developing an incredible boardwalk of independent retailers, and I just knew I had to be part of it.

That's where Elegant Touch Beauty was born. My vision was simple but ambitious: to create the most client-centric, salon experience possible. Somewhere people felt listened to, and truly valued.

But it wasn't going to be easy. The units were sought after, and to get the backing of the Marina, I had to present a business plan to the owners, John and Michael Thornton, former owners of Thorntons Chocolates. At the time, I didn't grasp how big a deal that was. Looking back now, I realise how young I was, and how much faith they placed in me.

The salon build from an empty shell was exhausting, but by the Summer of 2014 it was ready. My new home at Mercia Marina was finally complete. I had just turned 22 when I opened the doors. It was just me, no team, standing in a space I dreamed into existence. I was excited. I was terrified.

In those early days it was just hard work, no shortcuts. I found myself working seven days a week, pouring everything I had to make the salon a success. I didn't know if this was normal as I'd never owned a business before. But I felt a constant pressure to always be there, to always be doing something meaningful to push us forward, to never switch off.

My work life balance wasn't perfect, but the long hours and relentless drive was starting to pay off. Within three years, I was at capacity within the salon with a team of five. We had just been crowned Derbyshire New Business of the Year, a moment I won't ever forget. It was proof that we had built something special.

What made us special? The waterside views were breathtaking, aesthetics were fitting, but it was the way we treated our clients. We showed empathy, added thoughtful surprises, and cared beyond the treatment room. We hand-delivered gift vouchers, made home visits, and went out of our way to show our clients they mattered.

As momentum grew, we reinvested. We added advanced treatments: laser, skin tightening, microneedling, and more. It positioned us as a skincare destination. My team and I were growing together, pushing boundaries daily.

However, after the birth of my second daughter, everything changed. In late 2021, I suffered a mini-stroke and was left bed-bound for weeks. Up until that point, I'd kept up the relentless pace I'd always known.

It was terrifying. Lying there, I realised how close I'd come to losing everything, and for what? I'd been so focussed on proving I was 'good enough' that I'd forgotten to take care of myself.

That moment was the biggest wake-up call I ever had. To experience something so serious, so young, was a shock, but it forced me to reassess. I began listening to my body and stopped trying to do it all alone. I leaned into my team more, empowering others, and in doing so created something even stronger. It was a turning point that changed my approach not only to business, but to life.

It also provided me with an overwhelming feeling of perspective. It has resulted in me being even more in tune to the feelings of my team and clients, understanding that you have no idea what someone could be going through.

As time went on, the salon that once felt vast and empty was now alive with energy. We were fully booked, the team was growing, and the atmosphere was thriving. But I knew we had reached our limit. I was never going to compromise on the client experience, so it was time to find more space.

In 2024, the opportunity came. The largest retail unit at Mercia Marina, right next door to us, became available after the occupants decided to retire. A beautiful two-storey premises with amazing views across the water, four times our original size. I knew it was a risk but everything in me said I had to take it.

I had an unrivalled location, a loyal and growing client base, and most importantly, the most incredible team alongside me. My vision was clear: to double-down on everything we'd built and create a salon that's truly beautiful. My amazing team and clients deserved a location that wowed.

I was aware expectations would be high, but I wanted to exceed them. This time, I didn't pick up a paintbrush. I brought in a professional interior agency and guided them with my vision. Together, we created something breathtaking that reflects who we are now.

Originally, I thought growth would be slow and steady. But what happened next surprised me.

Recruitment, once daunting, suddenly felt effortless.

The more I invested into creating a space people genuinely wanted to be a part of, the more it attracted the right people. Therapists were turning up before we even opened with their CVs, drawn in by the vision. For the first time I saw how much of a magnet the right environment could be. In just three months, we grew from a team of five to a team of 12, ready and excited to open our doors together.

From the very start, I knew it was the little touches that would set us apart. We brought in a complimentary welcome tray with essential oils, biodegradable hand towel, and a sweet treat. Personalised name cards on the treatment beds. A beautiful, private, relaxation space looking over the water. Client goody bags. After care cards, and more.

They aren't just 'extras', they are intentional, powerful detail, to show clients how deeply we care. What I have learned is if you want to be the best, it's not about doing what everyone else is doing. Do what you believe in, and do it wholeheartedly.

Shortly after opening, applications opened for the Professional Beauty Awards 2025 and my husband began an application for the Large Salon category. We were only a couple of months in, but everything felt aligned.

The process was surprisingly therapeutic. As an owner, you're always in the moment or looking ahead. This gave me space to reflect on how far we had come. Over weeks, our journey was poured into that application.

We were selected as finalists. I was bowled over. To be standing alongside past winners, and some of the most established salons was a moment of pride, and reminded me just how far passion, belief, and hard work can take you.

But soon, that pride turned into determination: Now we have to win.

The judge's visit came quickly. Everything had been prepared down to the smallest detail, but butterflies were still fluttering.

The visit was wonderful. On one hand, it was our moment to showcase to a true industry leader what we had built, meet our team, and hear our journey. But on the other, it was a chance to learn, soak up their insight, and to simply share the moment with someone who understood what all this means.

My team were flawless that day, but I was unsure if I'd personally done enough. Perhaps I was too modest. Despite the high regard I have for everything we do; I don't always find it easy saying it. My inner doubt still lingers.

In March, the team and I travelled to London for the awards ceremony. The glitz, the nerves, the disbelief. It was all there.

Then it happened.

'And the winner is... Elegant Touch Beauty'. I'll never forget it. I dropped to my knees as our table erupted in celebration! It was euphoric. That announcement carried the weight of every late night, every moment of doubt. We had done it, together.

The weeks that followed were a whirlwind for all of us.

The business was propelled into a new territory. We conducted numerous media interviews, and Susan Routledge, who I had long admired, invited me on an episode of her podcast.

I've made an effort to embrace the opportunities that have come my way since, despite them taking me out of my comfort zone. Growth followed, not just for the business, but for me also.

So, what's next?

As I write this, we've just been named a finalist for Large Salon of the Year at the BABTAC Awards. It's an incredible honour. We've got everything crossed, but regardless of the outcome, the fire in my belly is still burning.

Elegant Touch Beauty has come so far. But the journey so far is just beginning. I'm more inspired than ever.

Top Tips

- Don't just copy others. Do what you believe in and do it with excellence.
- Find an outlet to escape. Mine is running. My morning run clears my head and gives me space to think clearly.
- Nurture your team as much as your clients. A happy, motivated team deliver exceptional client experiences.

Acknowledgements

My husband Dan. With me from the very beginning. My sounding board in the evenings, and support with the structure to allow my vision to flourish.

My two daughters. You are my purpose and why I strive to succeed.

About Anna Inglis

Anna Inglis is the visionary founder of Elegant Touch Beauty, an award-winning salon recognised for excellence in client care and attention to detail.

Since launching the business at age 22, Anna has expanded the salon into a premier two-storey location at Mercia Marina, growing her team from a solo operation to a talented team of 14.

Her leadership philosophy centres on building a happy, motivated team, knowing that exceptional staff drive outstanding client experiences. Anna places great importance on the small, thoughtful touches that elevate every visit, distinguishing Elegant Touch Beauty within a competitive market.

Under her direction, the salon has earned prestigious accolades including Derbyshire New Business of the Year, Large Salon of the Year at the Professional Beauty Awards, and finalist status for Large Salon of the Year at the BABTAC Awards.

Anna lives in Derby with her supportive husband, and two amazing daughters.

LinkedIn - https://www.linkedin.com/in/anna-inglis-8a33b6b3

Website - www.eleganttouchuk.co.uk

Facebook – www.facebook.com/ElegantTouchBeauty

Instagram – www.instagram.com/elegant_touch_beauty

Email – info@eleganttouchuk.co.uk

My Journey To Escape

Faye Lazarides

When someone asks me what advice I'd give to someone starting a business, I usually begin with this: be prepared for a journey that is anything but predictable. Business is a rollercoaster – full of highs, lows, learning curves, and unexpected turns. Passion is essential, but so are resilience, adaptability, and self-belief.

From a young age, I knew I wanted to run my own salon. I had a clear vision of creating a space where women felt cared for and confident—somewhere they could trust in the expertise and quality of service. I also had a natural inclination toward leadership. I was confident that I could manage a team, take ownership of a space, and grow something of my own.

My career in the beauty industry began early. At 17, I joined Regis, which later became the Urban Retreat at Harrods – one of the most prestigious beauty destinations in London at the time. I started as a nail technician, as Regis required five years of experience before allowing therapists to work in full beauty roles. However, when George Hammer, the owner of the Urban Retreat, took over the business, he introduced new opportunities. At just 19 years old, I stepped into the role of beauty therapist.

Working at Harrods offered invaluable exposure. I worked with exceptionally skilled colleagues and served a high-profile clientele. Within three years, I had moved into management and later expanded my role to oversee a broader territory. It was fast-paced, challenging, and rewarding—a strong foundation that shaped the way I approached both service and business.

After five years at Harrods, I took a position with La Prairie, a Swiss luxury skincare brand renowned for its high-performance products. The role was different and allowed me to explore another side of the industry. I traveled across the south of the UK, supporting brand managers in department stores, facilitating events, and performing treatments for clients. The role offered a new kind of independence and gave me insight into how luxury beauty brands operate at a regional level.

One of the highlights of that time was participating in the Lady Taverners event at Whatley Manor. Staying in one of their beautiful suites and dining in a Michelin-starred restaurant was an experience I'll always remember – it was a glimpse into the level of service and elegance I wanted to one day provide in my own business.

Eventually, the travel became unsustainable. I was newly married, and constantly being away from home began to take its toll. Fortunately, my manager at the time, Beverley, supported me in transitioning to a role at Peter Jones, another landmark department store in London. There, I assisted the account manager for the brand full time. While I appreciated the opportunity, the environment lacked the pace and scale I had grown accustomed to. It became clear to me that I needed a new direction.

That was the moment I knew it was time to start something of my own.

I had gained almost a decade of solid experience in beauty therapy, retail, luxury branding, management, and customer care. I had seen what worked, what didn't, and what truly elevated a client's experience. My brother Chris, already established in hairdressing, was Vidal Sassoon-trained and had also worked in many great salons – including the Urban Retreat at Harrods. He shared the same ambition.

Together, we decided to open our own salon.

I didn't have formal training in business – but I had practical experience, insight, and a clear vision. Starting out was challenging. There were mistakes, setbacks, and difficult decisions. But there were also milestones, growth, and a sense of purpose that made it all worthwhile.

After months of planning—finalising our business strategy, securing a loan, finding the right location, and choosing the brands we wanted to align with – Escape Hair and Beauty was born.

On October 2, 2007, my brother and I opened the doors to our very own salon. We stood there, filled with pride and excitement. It had all come together – a stunning, luxury space we had built from the ground up, right in the heart of Finchley Central. At that moment, it felt like we had arrived. We believed, without hesitation, that our success was inevitable.

Looking back now, I realise that opening the doors wasn't the end of the dream – it was only the beginning.

Our first week in business brought a sharp wake-up call. We were fined for not informing our landlord – in writing – about changing the shopfront signage. It seemed like a minor oversight, especially considering it felt obvious we would want to put our name above the door.

But buried in the fine print of our contract was a clause we'd missed. No one had pointed it out, and we paid the price.

Shortly after, the UK was hit with its biggest financial crisis in decades. The 2008 recession cast a long shadow across businesses nationwide. At 24, with my personal property tied to the business, it shook me to my core. I had taken a massive risk. The fear was real. But I was also fiercely determined – we would survive this. We had to.

Despite the uncertainty, our business began to thrive. We built a team of talented, kind-hearted staff – some of whom I still look back on with real warmth. Our client base grew steadily, and the salon gained a strong reputation for professionalism and care. Outwardly, we were doing well. But beneath the surface, I carried a constant pressure. A quiet, persistent voice asking: Can we really hold this all together?

Around this time, my personal life was evolving rapidly. I had recently married, and two years into running the salon, my husband and I decided to start a family. That journey began painfully, with a miscarriage. It was a devastating loss, made harder by the relentless pace I was keeping up in the business. I had little time or space to process what I was going through. The stress was constant, and it took a toll on my health – mentally and physically.

A year later, our daughter Elyscia was born. She was everything. Perfect in every way. Becoming a mother changed me – but it came with its own set of challenges. Within the space of four years, I had experienced a lot. It was a whirlwind.

Elyscia was born via emergency C-section, and within five weeks, I was back at work. I'd been told I wasn't entitled to maternity leave because our business was still new.

The recession was still looming, and the pressure to be present at the salon weighed heavily on me. But so did the guilt of leaving my newborn at home. I felt torn – unable to fully commit to either role without feeling like I was failing in the other.

Those early years were anything but easy. But they were deeply formative.

If there's one lesson I've carried with me from that time, it's this:

Be clear about your goals– but understand that very little will go to plan.

You will need strength, persistence, and flexibility.

There will be setbacks. There will be emotional strain. But you are more capable than you know.

And even when it feels like you're barely holding it together – you are doing it.

No business – no dream – is ever built without challenges. The key is to keep going.

As the years passed, I began to realise something incredibly reassuring – our business was not only growing, it was stable.

What started as a leap of faith had evolved into a trusted name in our community. We had built a loyal and supportive clientele, many of whom are still with us nearly two decades later. That kind of loyalty doesn't happen by accident. It comes from consistency, care, and genuine relationships.

Of course, the challenges didn't end once we were established.

In 2015, my husband and I welcomed our second child, our son Christian. Balancing business ownership with motherhood once again required careful juggling – especially with a young daughter already at home. But by this point, I had learned how to adapt. I understood the importance of having the right support around me, both personally and professionally.

Then came 2020 the COVID-19 pandemic. Like so many businesses in the beauty industry, we were forced to close our doors for months. It was one of the most uncertain periods we had ever faced. Yet somehow, we navigated through. The strength of our client relationships, our reputation, and the foundation we'd worked so hard to build helped us weather the storm.

In the years that followed, we made the decision to relocate the salon—a move that felt both daunting and exciting. But it proved to be the right choice. With change came renewed energy, new opportunities, and a fresh chapter in our journey.

Looking back, I see a business built not just on skills and treatments, but on perseverance, adaptability, and a deep commitment to people.

We survived economic downturns, personal loss, a global pandemic, and the unpredictable demands of life—and we're still here. Stronger. Wiser. More rooted in purpose than ever before.

About Faye Lazarides

Faye Lazarides is a highly qualified beauty industry professional with over 25 years of experience in luxury skincare, salon management, and customer experience. Starting her career at 17 with the prestigious Urban Retreat at Harrods, she quickly rose through the ranks, gaining invaluable insights into high-end service and brand excellence.

In 2007, she co-founded Escape Hair and Beauty with her brother, creating a space rooted in professionalism, care, and community. Through economic downturns, personal loss, motherhood, and a global pandemic, she has grown her business with resilience and heart.

Her journey is a testament to grit, passion, and an unwavering belief in her vision. Today, she continues to inspire as a business owner and advocate for women balancing business with everyday life. This is her story – honest, hard-earned, and deeply human.

Instagram: fayes_beauty_room

https://www.instagram.com/fayes_beauty_room

From Lambing Season To Laser Clinics: A Journey of Finding My Niche

Marie Drummond

My story begins not in a bustling city or a bright salon, but in the soft rolling hills of the countryside, where the mornings start before the sun rises and the mist hangs low over the fields. It was there, on a family farm, that I grew up—quiet, observant, and surrounded by the rhythm of nature.

I was a shy child, happiest in the stillness of early mornings. The farm could be chaotic at times, but there was something sacred about the hours before the world woke. My favourite time of year was always lambing season. While other children might have dreaded the cold or the mess, I looked forward to it with all my heart. There was something magical about helping new life into the world—watching a tiny lamb take its first breath under the warm watch of a heat lamp or gently rubbing life into a weak newborn beside my father.

My dad and I shared those precious dawn hours together, walking among the pens, checking on the ewes, offering silent comfort where needed. It's in those quiet mornings is where my dad would teach and show me all there was to know about farming. I learned by watching.

Those mornings gave me a sense of purpose, a kind of peace I didn't find anywhere else.

But as I grew older, the safe cocoon of the farm gave way to the unfamiliar world of school. From the very beginning, it felt like I was somehow falling behind. While other children rattled off spelling tests and read aloud with ease, I struggled. Letters seemed to dance on the page, refusing to stay in line. I'd dread being called on to read out loud – the way the room would go quiet, all eyes on me as I stumbled and hesitated over words everyone else seemed to understand.

Retaining information was like trying to catch smoke with my hands. Teachers mistook my quietness and struggle as lack of intelligence, and I began to believe it myself. Still, I worked harder than most, and with quiet resilience, I pushed on.

It wasn't until college that someone finally looked closer and said the word that changed everything: dyslexia. Suddenly, the years of struggle made sense. I wasn't slow or broken I just processed the world differently. That diagnosis didn't erase the challenges, but it gave me understanding, and from that came confidence.

Around that time, I found a different kind of passion – one rooted not in livestock or textbooks, but in wellness and self-care. I started training in beauty therapy, drawn to the way it could make people feel – not just physically better, but more confident, more seen.

My career began in spas, working in places like Centre Parcs and eventually the prestigious spa "The Mere" in Knutsford. There, I worked with world-renowned brands such as Elemis and Decléor, learning not just the techniques but the art of care. I studied people's skin, their energy, their stories.

I found a gift for connecting without many words, much like those early mornings on the farm with my dad.

But something inside me wanted more. I dreamed of working for myself, even if the idea terrified me. I started small – renting space in the back rooms of hair salons, juggling treatments in cramped quarters. I printed leaflets and walked door to door, rain or shine, slipping them through letterboxes praying my hard work would pay off.

I offered everything – waxing, nails, facials, massages – anything to grow my little business. Slowly, appointment by appointment, I built trust, and with it, a loyal client base. Every thank you, every rebooking felt like a small triumph.

Eventually, the time came to take a bigger step. I signed the lease on my very first salon. It was a huge moment – scary, exciting, overwhelming. And then, life threw me another curveball: I found out I was pregnant with my second child. My first was only two years old. The timing couldn't have been more intense – but something in me said, *You've got this*.

That "something" came, in part, from my mum. She wasn't one for big speeches or emotional pep talks – but she was always there. Whether it was helping me hand out leaflets when I first started working for myself, or quietly looking after my children while I treated clients, she showed up without question. She never asked for recognition, never made it about her – but her support was constant and steady, woven into every step I took.

At six months pregnant, with swollen ankles and a heart full of determination, I invested in my very first laser device. That decision changed everything. I began to specialize – no longer offering every treatment under the sun, but instead focusing on advanced skin therapies. I carved out a niche where science met skincare, and passion met purpose.

Since that first laser machine, I've continued to invest in cutting-edge technology – High-Intensity Focused Ultrasound (HIFU), Radio Frequency Microneedling, LED light therapy, and more. Each tool became an extension of my desire to help people feel confident in their own skin, to give them real results with care and integrity.

Now, two decades into the beauty industry and two years into owning my thriving salon, I look back with pride. I've balanced building a business with growing a family – managing sleepless nights and toddler tantrums with client consultations and skin transformation plans.

And among all those milestones, one stands out like a quiet exclamation mark: winning the PHAB Advanced Service Star Award. To be recognised not just for my technical skill, but for the care and service I provide—that was a moment I'll never forget. It felt like the world saw me for who I really was. I was the second person in the UK to receive this award, and to this day, only two of us hold that honour. That recognition filled me with pride—not just for what I had achieved, but for how I had done it: with heart, integrity, and a genuine love for helping others feel confident in their own skin.

I've learned that success doesn't always come loud or fast. Sometimes, it's quiet and slow and deeply rooted—just like the mornings on the farm where my story began. I'm proud of how far I've come: from the shy girl who struggled to find her voice in a crowded classroom, to a woman who built a thriving business, guided by compassion, determination, and a quiet belief in something more.

To any beauty therapist standing where I once stood – wondering if they're good enough, or capable enough – I want to say this: nothing is out of your reach.

Trust yourself. You are capable of more than you know. Start small if you need to, take imperfect steps, but never stop believing that you can build something beautiful.

Plus, don't be afraid to ask for help. You don't have to do everything on your own.

We all have different strengths – lean on others who are experts in areas you're not. Whether it's outsourcing your social media, getting help with accounting, or bringing in a business mentor – getting the right support is not a sign of weakness; it's a smart step forward. Don't try to wear every hat or carry every task until you burn out. You deserve to grow your business and still have space for yourself.

Every challenge has shaped me. Every setback has strengthened me. And every step – whether on muddy farmland or polished salon floors – has brought me closer to a life filled with meaning, connection, and purpose.

Today, as I stand in my own clinic, surrounded by clients I care deeply about and treatments I believe in, I no longer question my place in the world. I've found my niche – not just in laser clinics or skincare, but in helping others feel seen, valued, and confident.

And while the journey here has had its share of twists and turns, I know one thing for certain: I'm not done growing. This is only the beginning of what I'm capable of. The farm taught me patience, beauty therapy taught me connection, and motherhood taught me strength. With all of that in my heart – I'm ready for whatever comes next.

About Marie Drummond

Marie has worked in the beauty industry for 20 years, starting with a wide range of treatments—nails, waxing, massage, and facials—before discovering her true passion in advanced skin care. The journey hasn't been without challenges. Diagnosed with dyslexia later in life, she struggled throughout school, often feeling left behind. But those early setbacks built my resilience and drive to succeed. Over time, she found her niche in skin health and now specialise in transformative treatments using cutting-edge technologies like HIFU, radiofrequency microneedling, IPL facials, and many more. After years of working in top spas including Centre Parcs and The Mere, she took the leap and opened my own clinic. Now, two years into running her own salon, she has created a space where science, care, and confidence come together. Her goal is simple: to help people feel truly seen, valued, and radiant in their skin—because she knows what it means to be overlooked.

Website: botanicbeautyrooms.com

Email: botanicbeautyrooms@hotmail.com

Instagram: https://www.instagram.com/

You're Never Too Late, Too Old Or Too Broken To Start Again

Carole Lacey

I have always been captivated by the idea of flawless skin, not out of vanity, but because I felt I had something to cover up. At 18, I was painfully self-conscious about my red, inflamed complexion. Makeup became my mask and my shield, a way to feel safe in my own skin. I didn't know then that I had rosacea, a skin condition that can now be treated quite successfully.

So, you can imagine the panic I felt when I was invited to a skincare and makeup evening at my friend's house. Take off my makeup in front of everyone? Absolutely not! I told her. I agreed to go but stay in the background. But something unexpected happened that night. Over the course of the evening, I became completely mesmerised, I found myself being drawn in by the consultant, the way in which she spoke so naturally and confidently. She transformed her model's dull, tired skin right before our eyes. It lit something in me. When she announced she was recruiting new trainees, I didn't hesitate. I dipped into my savings, bought the kit, and stepped, heart first, into my new career.

After completing my three-month training as a beauty consultant, I kept my day job in the office, but by night I became a travelling beauty advisor, offering skincare guidance and teaching makeup techniques to women who, like me, simply wanted to feel confident and comfortable in their own skin.

I became a go-to for brides and their mums, but they didn't just want the makeup, they wanted the glow that started months before the big day, so I spoke to my bank manager (we had one in those days), and he encouraged me to train further in what I loved most. I gave up my office job and enrolled as a beauty therapy student, earning my CIBTAC and ITEC qualifications in beauty therapy. I spent two years absorbing everything I could, then returned to the road full time, only now with shiny new badges proudly pinned to my crisp white tunic dress.

Working as a mobile therapist had its rewards, but I craved more, a salon to shape and call my own. A place where my treatments could grow roots and my clients could feel completely at ease.

One afternoon, I passed a small shopfront tucked away on a quiet street. The light hit it exactly right, it felt like it was quietly calling to me. The energy, the size, the warmth, it was perfect. Then I saw the sign in the window: "Under Offer" Still, I couldn't shake the feeling. "That space is mine", I kept thinking.

I followed my instinct, found out who the landlord was and couldn't believe it was my old boss from when I was seventeen. He had once written me a glowing reference, so I sent it back to him, framed and signed. Within weeks, the keys were mine. My sanctuary was no longer a dream, it was real.

From the moment I opened the door, I poured my heart into that little salon. It wasn't just a workplace; it was my haven. Over the next twenty-five years, I built something truly special. Ivory Health & Beauty grew into a thriving space with a team of eight incredible therapists and a wonderfully loyal client base.

The business flourished so much that I opened a second salon in a nearby town, this time with a dedicated training centre to support my newest venture: a distribution business introducing non-invasive electrolysis to salons across the UK. I was travelling, training, mentoring, and expanding my reach far beyond the treatment room. To be at the forefront of beauty innovation was nothing short of thrilling.

And during it all, behind the scenes I was also raising two incredible boys as a single mum. There were school runs, sick days, sports matches, all carefully slotted between staff meetings and business travel. Looking back, I'm still not entirely sure how I managed it, but somehow, I did. It wasn't always graceful, and it certainly wasn't easy, but love, purpose and a deep-rooted sense of independence carried me through. My boys were my reason, my anchor. They grounded me in the chaos and gave everything I was building, a greater meaning.

Those years taught me resilience, the kind you don't read about in textbooks. I learned how to hold space for others while holding everything together at home. And through it all, I never lost sight of why I began: to help people feel better in their skin and ultimately in their lives.

That chapter of my life was full, busy, and beautiful. But, as fulfilling as it was, a quiet voice began to whisper again, a longing for stillness, connection, and something more soulful. That's when I enrolled in an Ayurvedic skincare training course. It felt like a homecoming, an opportunity to return to the treatment room with fresh eyes. During the course, I met a soft-spoken holistic therapist from Devon. We bonded instantly. I remember, she struggled to remove my makeup during her cleanse routine, until I explained it was tattooed on. We burst into giggles, not exactly ideal during a relaxing holistic facial.

When the course ended, we agreed to meet again. I drove 200 miles to visit her and tattooed her eyeliner. That trip changed everything. Standing by the sea, I felt something unexpected: overwhelming joy and a deep sense of freedom. I knew my boys needed more than concrete playgrounds and computer screens. They needed space, salt air, and adventure. Within six months, we'd bought a home in South Devon, and I opened my third clinic, this time in Kingsbridge, South Devon.

For a while, I tried to juggle it all, two salons, 200 miles apart and a life stretched thinly across the map. The boys were in boarding school, so I threw everything into the business driving over 400 miles per week, sometimes more, I was constantly on the move, living out of my car, racing from one salon to the next. It felt like I was chasing success… but losing myself in the process. No time for friends or family, just work, exhaustion, and endless stretches of motorway. I was running on fumes, physically and emotionally.

The more I pushed, the more I unravelled. Something had to change. I felt it in my heart.

It was time to let go. The business I had poured my heart into, the one that had felt like my first baby all those years ago, was ready for its next chapter. And so was I.

Then, unexpectedly, one of my team members offered to buy my business in Bourne End. I was overjoyed and felt an enormous sense of relief. We kept the deal quiet to protect staff and clients – until just four weeks before the exchange, when it collapsed. Word had somehow got out. Clients reframed from booking. Staff grew anxious. My dream began to crumble.

I tried to hold it all together, but with rising overheads, a shrinking team and a full life in Devon calling me, I had to make a choice.

After six months of struggle, I picked up the phone. I called my cousin, who owned a nearby hair and beauty salon, and offered her the business for £5,000. She knew it had once been worth £75,000

I remember standing in front of the mirror, asking myself, "Carole, what have you done?" Twenty-five years of hard work! My security, the memories, my parents' support - a huge part of that journey. But then, a quiet voice inside me spoke: "You're not selling your purpose. You're just letting go of some bricks and mortar." That voice saved me. I was 47, broke, but free. I had faith that I could do it all again!

My boys, then just teenagers, were thriving, surfing, laughing. Soaking up their new life and becoming the happiest I had ever seen them. That gave me the courage to begin again. I took out a loan, rolled up my sleeves, and poured everything I had into my new life in Devon.

At the time, my work: laser hair removal, semi-permanent makeup, chemical peels, and advanced skin treatments were relatively unknown in the region. But my 25 years of experience spoke volumes. Clients came. Word spread. I soon realised I needed a team again! I reinvested in new staff. I mentored them, trained them, encouraged them. Watching them grow professionally and personally was such a joy. This dynamic approach paid dividends as our continuous training kept us at the forefront of the industry.

Then came 2020. The world stood still, like for so many others I was forced to pause and reflect. My team had moved on, some into motherhood, others into new careers. I was at a crossroads: should I rebuild the business again... or go deeper, more personal, more aligned with my heart.

I chose me. I went it alone.

I opened a private clinic close to home, trained in liquid Microneedling, mesotherapy, radiofrequency, pulse-triggered laser therapy and advanced blemish removal, such powerful tools for real skin transformation, trained in cancer care facials and holistic massage techniques. A combination of Tech and Touch. I even launched a new website to sell skincare and wellness products online, giving clients access to results-driven skin routines at home.

I've never lost the nurturing side to my work. In fact, it's grown stronger. My clients say my treatments feel both futuristic and soulful. That's the magic. That's why I've become known locally as 'The Fairy Skin Mother'.

I have always believed that beautiful skin is an inside job, it begins with trust. My clients, many of whom are well-known in our community, come not only for results, but for the sanctuary I've created. A place where their skin is seen, heard, and celebrated.

Surrounding myself with the best in the industry gave me the confidence to step into the spotlight. I entered the BABTAC and Professional Beauty Awards and became a finalist four times. That milestone marked my forty years in the industry.

Since then, I've launched my own skin and wellness magazine, raised money for local charities, and introduced Skin Transformation Retreat Days at five-star hotels across Devon. These events go beyond skincare, they are about education, connection, and inspiration.

Through it all, I've pushed aside the voice of self-doubt, the inner critic that whispers you're too old or it's too late. Recently, someone told me I'm eligible to draw my pension. I smiled. Really? I'm just getting started.

So, this isn't just my story, it's a reminder to anyone reading this that you are never too late, too old, or too broken to start again. Your passion, your presence, your healing touch, that's the business. The bricks may fall. The tides may change. But if your heart is in it, you will rise again. Resilience, self-belief and staying true to yourself will be your superpower.

To every therapist who's lost their footing, every mother who's wondered if she's doing enough, and every woman who's quietly rebuilding their world - this chapter is for you.

For me, as I move into this next phase of my work life, I feel more inspired than ever to evolve not just as a facialist, but as a guide, a mentor, and a storyteller. I've learned that our skin doesn't just reflect what we put on it, but what we carry within it. The quiet weight of stress, the pace of our days, the emotions we tuck away, all leave their trace. My hope is to help women soften into themselves, embrace the grace of ageing, and reconnect with who they truly are. Because beauty isn't about chasing the past – it's about finding strength, softness, and confidence in your now.

About Carole Lacey

Carole Lacey, affectionately known as The Fairy Skin Mother, is a multi award-winning advanced facialist and founder of Waterside Aesthetics.

With over 40 years of experience, she blends cutting-edge, non-invasive technology with a holistic, nurturing approach to skincare. Based in Kingsbridge, South Devon, Carole offers personalised skin transformation journeys and Skin & Soul Retreats that help women feel confident and radiant at every stage of life.

A respected industry mentor and educator, she's built and led thriving beauty businesses and inspired countless aspiring therapists. Her story is one of reinvention, purpose, and the belief that beauty should be celebrated at every age.

When she's not in treatment, Carole can be found walking her beloved Siberian Husky, Sansha, along the beach or swimming in the sea—where she feels most at home.

www.watersideaesthetics.com

https://www.instagram.com/waterside.aesthetics

carole@watersideaesthetics.com

www.skin-solutions.online and info@skin-solutions.online

https://www.instagram.com/skin_solutions

https://www.instagram.com/skinandsoulretreat

Penguin On The Cliff

Cheryl Eager

My name is Cheryl, and I was fortunate enough to be born into a farming family in Cheshire. I had a happy childhood playing outside with lots of animals, making dens in the hay and straw barn with friends from the village. I was always very social and loved being at school.

When I was 11, my Dad got an indoor market stall selling handbags and jewellery, which my mum ran. Farming was already beginning to struggle, even back then, and he could not understand why Mum needed yet another bag for any social occasion, or the answer *'you really can't go to a wedding with the same old handbag!'* We used to sit around the kitchen table at night, my brother included, pricing the jewellery and bags, and on Saturdays, I worked on the stall.

I enjoyed senior school, but was always a bit slow at picking things up and struggled with numbers. I always seemed to get them the wrong way round. Like most teenagers, I was terribly self-conscious and always felt overweight (Twiggys' fault!), with my lack of self-confidence, being a people pleaser came easily to me.

When it came to deciding what I would do on leaving school, I was petrified as I knew I was no academic. I just wanted to be with people and help them. Could I be a nurse? Not me, it would be way too upsetting. I really wanted to learn how to apply makeup properly, so as a birthday treat, Mum booked me a group lesson with Estee Lauder, and that was it! I was hooked!

I figured that there must be lots of people just like me, who needed direction with their make up, so I wrote to the Barbara Daly School of make up, I just didn't tell anyone, so when the school phoned to speak to me Mum was flabbergasted, anyway it ended up we had a trip to London to investigate.

It was obvious to the lovely ladies there that I was as green as the fields we had left in Cheshire, and they told us about Beauty Therapy training, which we were not aware of. Mum only had her hair done, and there were no beauty salons in our area (how times have changed).

This opened a new world to me, and I was lucky enough to go to The Lilllan Maund School of Beauty Therapy in Marple, which later moved to Stockport. I loved it! It was so very strict, and if you didn't pass inspection first thing in the morning, you were not allowed into the class; you would have to rectify whatever the problem was, i.e. nails, makeup up or hair, and join the class at the first break. You had the same penalty if you dared to be late. I enjoyed every minute of the training and was very nervous about the exams. But I got there and on completion of the Cidesco exam I cried all the way home.

My first job was at a small health farm at Ellel Grange, Lancashire, which I enjoyed very much. I then moved closer to home and worked at a lovely home salon in Northwich, Cheshire, which wasn't dissimilar to my business now. The salon owner was a lovely lady who was great to work for; she was so glamorous and looked like she was from the set of *Dallas*, but I was bored and had always wanted to travel.

I had an application form for the ships form in my bedside cabinet for over a year until I plucked up the courage to send it. This was my first penguin on the cliff moment, the picture of the penguin that looks as though he is hanging on the edge of the cliff before it leaps. Yes, that's me!

The ship's interview was in London and was the only interview that Mum never came to, as she did not want me to work away. Needless to say, I got the job and off I went to join my first ship in Puerto Rico. I got out of the taxi, saw the ship, and my heart fell through the ground! What had I done? When I saw my cabin, what no portholes? No daylight? Oh my word, how was I going to last? I was fine, I loved it, loved the work, which were very long hours, loved waking in a different port each day, and of course just adored being with and meeting lots of different people.

To work on the ships, I was required to be trained in Guinot, which was the first real skincare company I had trained with, and I thought it was just wonderful, I still do.

I left the ships to be with and marry a boyfriend, which brought me to Brighton. I was dreadfully homesick. The marriage was not great, nor was Brighton for me. Sadly, I left my much-loved beauty therapy for a few years. We got a pub in Shoreham-by-Sea where I felt I could settle, which I have, and I am still here 36 years later.

The marriage broke down, and I was lucky enough to initially get work as a receptionist at a beautiful clinic in The Lanes in Brighton. I quickly started to carry out treatments and was fortunate enough to be sent on a Decleor training course, which was wonderful. I loved my facials, and the products were amazing. After three years, it was time to move on. I found employment in Hove at a larger salon, with more staff. Here I went back to working with Guinot, Decleor, adding Caci, Jan Marini and Environ to my repertoire. My boss was great, as were the girls; we were a very happy and busy salon. I had also remarried at this time.

After several years, I was beginning to get itchy feet and was aware that I was the eldest therapist in the salon. I didn't want to be the old therapist in the corner room, who was always a bit behind and a bit slow. Another *penguin* moment coming up, I had always fancied taking Guinot to Shoreham, nearer to where I lived, but way too scared. The old self-confidence thing again. Eventually, I did the penguin leap off the cliff and rented a small room above Fox and Sons in Shoreham town centre.

I was exceptionally lucky that my beautiful boss told me that I could tell my very regular clients I was leaving and where I was going, which was so very generous of her.

The building where I rented my room was a modern building, on an older site commonly known, in the day, as the Vinery. Beauty at the Vinery was born!

I had Guinot as my skincare line, non-surgical face lifting, Australian tea tree wax, and OPI nailcare. I worked every hour there was and my business gradually built up, which was great as I had no shop front, just an A-board on the pavement down below.

The years went on, and one day, one of my lovely clients asked me what plans I had for the Vinery. Survival, I thought to myself. She asked if I had ever thought of a business partner? Well, no! I thought. So I was rather amazed that she was asking me.

Toni had been my most regular client from Hove and had supported me unstintingly when I became self-employed, buying everyone she knew vouchers for birthdays and Christmas.

I really was flabbergasted. Why was she asking me? So many other therapists and salons out there? Yes, the old self-confidence thing again. So we arranged a lunch date at her place in Hove for me to take my accounts for her to look at. She prepared a lovely lunch, and I honestly thought that once she had looked at my accounts, she would not really be interested. We decided that during the summer, Toni would come in to help at the desk and see how we got on and how she liked the business. Tonis' background was very different from mine; she had worked and grown up in London, working mainly in marketing, and was extremely successful. So high-flyer city girl unites with small village country bumpkin girl! We got on so well and she helped me enormously, we became and still are very firm friends.

By now, we were looking at expanding and taking more rooms. Sadly, at that time, there were no decent properties to rent in the town, so we were stuck. Toni hit on the idea of buying somewhere to live and work from, I thought she was bonkers, but that is actually what happened.

We let our old house and bought a house on the main road into Shoreham with ample space for parking, always important in a growing town. Another *penguin* moment, would we get a change of use for the property? Would we get the mortgage? Would the clients stay with us? Would the timings of it all work out? very stressful! Yes, it did all happen, and within two weeks Tonis' partner rebuilt all the downstairs, decorated, and we moved house and business over the weekend. We worked on the Saturday in the old rooms and opened on the Monday in the new salon. It was fabulous, the rooms are beautiful, a decent size, and two of them with lovely big windows overlooking the garden at the front of the house. Following the move, we became The Vinery Beauty Clinic.

I still really love the name and our logo.

We went from strength to strength and had a good team of therapists working with us. We used to go to the local airshow when Guinot sponsored the wing walkers, where we got to promote the salon. It was so much fun, but even though we were busy, we were not making lots of money, so many challenges had to be looked at, pricing structure, wages, PAYE, and it goes on. Moving on, we have overcome recessions, hard times, and staff issues, but we are still here, stronger than ever, moving forward. Another penguin moment is looming, except this time I will be happily leaping off the cliff with my self-belief intact and Toni by my side.

For me, a determination to push through and self-belief are so important. Loving my work and our beautiful clients is so fulfilling. Toni and I had a wonderful experience recently, one of our clients' Dads had come to collect her with her baby, whom we were eager to meet. I felt so proud that we used to do Grandma's treatments, still do Mum and daughters treatments, and here was the fourth generation visiting us, not that we will be around to be doing her treatments! We are so proud of our journey; we have laughed and cried on this journey. And...

There is still a lot more to come!

About Cheryl Eager

Cheryl Eager (nee Morris) lives in West Sussex, having grown up on a small farm in Cheshire. After attending Beauty School, gaining CIDESCO, British Confederation and ITEC certificates in Beauty Therapy, massage and electrolysis, worked in the Beauty industry, also on cruise ships for some years.

After working in Brighton and Hove, she decided to open a salon in her hometown of Shoreham-by-Sea, where she still practices with her business partner Toni Frazier, who manages the salon and the marketing aspect of the business, leaving Cheryl to do what she most prefers, which is treatments and looking after her much-loved clients.

Cheryl still has a passion for animals and the countryside from her childhood and always has s dog companion by her side, and is also active in the community of Shoreham by Sea

Web: www.thevinerybeautyclinic.com

Email: thevinerybeautyclinic@gmail.com

https:/www.facebook.com/TheVineryBeautyClinic/info

Let Nothing Stand in Your Way

Lucie McHugo

I wasn't academic, my highest achievement at school was an 'A' in Art and I had no clue what I wanted to do when I left. My mom suggested business administration, so following my sister's footsteps I went to college. I worked in an office and at the age of 25 I fell pregnant with my eldest son. Whilst on maternity leave the company folded and I was made redundant. Soon after, when my son was just 15 months old, I split with his dad. The relationship had been volatile, so I knew it was for the best.

I moved back in with my parents. My mom was my rock. She gave me the strength to rebuild. I had decided that I was the one who was going to provide for me and my son. I didn't want to go back to office work, it just didn't fulfil me. I needed something with purpose.

That's when I decided to go back to college to train in Beauty Therapy. I enrolled at Bournville college to start Level 2 Beauty Therapy, while I waited for the course to begin, I took an evening Indian Head Massage class. I loved it. I felt alive for the first time in a long time. Helping people feel better about themselves lit something in me. I'd found my passion.

I threw myself into learning, I enrolled in Reflexology, Anatomy

& Physiology, alongside Beauty Therapy. I was fascinated by the skin and the body. I could see a vision of the future, and for the first time, I felt excited. I knew I wanted to run my own business.

I studied Level 3 Beauty Therapy while working at AVEDA in House of Fraser, then in an AVEDA spa. I even exchanged admin work for room rent at a local holistic practice. I was soaking up everything, I learned about the full client journey, from the moment they walked through the door to how they felt after they left. I wanted to make people feel comfortable and at ease, I wanted to make a difference, no matter what they were going through at the time. I knew this was in preparation for when I was ready to run my own business.

I carried on to do Foundation Degree in Salon Business Management at UCB Birmingham and became interested in aesthetics. Nearing 30, I started feeling self-conscious about my own appearance. I thought I was getting "old", I laugh about it now. I wanted Botox for my frown lines and maybe filler for my lip, which had been uneven since my childhood skateboard accident. I was searching for perfection.

I found a well-known clinic in Edgbaston and booked a consultation. The consultant offered to do the procedure there and then. I agreed, trusting her as the expert. But it went wrong. The nurse injected filler on the side I'd said not to. My lip swelled massively where I had scar tissue, it reacted badly, I was mortified. I couldn't speak to anyone. I avoided going out, hid my face, and lost confidence. The clinic offered to dissolve it (with the risk of flesh-eating allergic reaction!) or top up the other side. I was naive and scared it would react so chose the latter, it made things worse.

Years later, a kind and trusted nurse helped me corrected it.

That experience scarred me deeply, but it taught me so much. I knew then that I didn't want to go into aesthetics, I NEVER wanted ANYONE to go through what I went through and feel the way I had. That was the moment my purpose became crystal clear: to help people feel confident, naturally.

Around this time, my mom started getting back pain. A month after my 30th birthday, she was diagnosed with terminal lung cancer that had spread to her spine. My world came crashing down. My dad had just been given the 12 month all-clear from prostate cancer, how could this be happening again? I remember my mom saying, "What are we going to do without your dad?" And now, here we were, asking the same about her. She was only 64. How were we going to get through this?

I had to dig deep and be positive and strong for her, just as she had always been for me. As a family, we pulled together. She was in and out of hospital, we nursed her at home, but just two months later, she passed away. She never shed a tear. She was strong until the end.

I finished my second year at uni because I knew she'd want me to. She never got to see me graduate. It took a long time to come to terms with her passing. My eldest son was four years old at the time, we were still living at home with my parents. He gave me and my dad a reason to keep going. For his sake, we had to carry on. I had a week off work but found it was a good distraction to go back to work as I only worked part time.

A few years later, I was offered the chance to rent a room and finally start my beauty business. It was a dream come true. I invested in a CACI machine and focused on advanced facials and beauty treatments. After my ordeal with lip filler, I knew non-invasive treatments were the way forward. I fell in love with 'skin' and how it helped make people feel good about their appearance in a natural, non-invasive way. My diary quickly filled up. I was flying, but I burned out.

That Christmas, I worked right up until Christmas Eve and woke up ill on Christmas Day. I had pushed too hard and my body had had enough. That was my wake-up call. I realised I couldn't keep up this peace, it wasn't sustainable. I needed to take care of myself. Since then, I've made it a rule not to work Christmas Eve, and I've learned to take time out when I need it. I used to believe that being busy meant being successful, but now I know that success means having a work life balance.

Later, I met my two younger two sons. He swept me off my feet and promised he'd look after me and my eldest and take him on as his own. He proposed to me in Venice and we married in Dubai. It looked perfect from the outside. I had two sons, 16 months apart, both born by C-section. I was back to work six weeks after having them, trying not to let my clients down and to keep the business that I had built going. I worked from home, squeezing in clients between breastfeeding. But behind closed doors, things were falling apart.

He drank heavily, which led to arguments. He pushed my family away, even my eldest son, who eventually chose to live with his dad. I was devastated and heartbroken. I tried to keep everything together, raising two babies, running a business, I was crumbling inside. No one knew. I stayed professional at work, creating a warm and welcoming atmosphere for my clients while my own world was falling apart.

Then came lockdown. Things got worse. My husband wouldn't let my eldest visit. I messaged him every night. We'd go for walks just to see each other. It shattered me inside. When my son asked to stay, and my husband said no, I knew I had to act.

I called Women's Aid. My caseworker was incredible. I began

legal proceedings and got the court orders I needed. A friend, Michelle Smith, helped me every step of the way. One day she prayed for me, something shifted. I found the strength to pack a suitcase and leave with my two youngest boys. We stayed in a women's refuge for six weeks until my ex moved out under an occupation order.

During that time, I continued working from home when restrictions allowed. The rules kept changing. We were allowed to work, then we weren't, but I stayed professional and focused on making people feel better during a very uncertain time. I think people really needed their treatments then, not just to get their nails done or to have a facial, but for connection and normality. I told no one what was going on apart from my dad and Michelle. I'll never forget what they did for me. I'm especially grateful to Michelle for believing in me and standing by me, I wouldn't be where I am today without her!

When I returned home, I began the process of rebuilding. One of the most important parts was reconnecting with my eldest son. Finally, we could be a family again and he could stay over whenever he wanted. I took the younger children to a contact centre to see their dad whilst we were going to court for child arrangements. I divorced on the grounds of 'controlling and coercive behaviour', finally I was free. My dad was amazing and stepped in to help with the boys.

When lockdown lifted, I reopened my business and began renting a room in a hair salon. Bit by bit, I started to find my feet again. I loved being back in the salon after working from home while the boys were babies. I remember thinking how lovely it was to see people again. Slowly, I started to find my spark after what had been such a long and strange time, but I had no vision, I didn't know which direction to take my business.

I found Susan Routledge and the Beauty Directors Club. I gained clarity and focus to move my business forward. Now, I run a thriving skin clinic. I focus on real results and real confidence. I want my clients to feel good inside and out. I believe in loving yourself first, because if I had, I might not have stayed so long in an abusive relationship.

Most people don't know the full story. I never wanted pity. I'm not a victim. I'm proud of who I am today. Stronger. Wiser. Resilient. Everything I've been through has shaped me. I wouldn't change it. It gave me my boys. It gave me purpose.

Today, I'm happy. I've met someone kind and caring. It took time to trust again, especially with my boys. I'm proud of my journey. Sometimes I look back and think, "Did that really happen to me?" It did. And it made me.

My story isn't one of defeat, it's one of strength, survival, and passion. You don't have to wait until you're fully healed to decide who you want to be. The past doesn't define you. When life throws a curveball, choose your future. Show up with consistency and clarity. You are in control.

Today I help people glow with confidence from the inside out, as beauty starts within. I don't want anyone to feel the way I felt at the start of my journey. I want to support their skin transformation journey, to give them the confidence to live the life they've always dreamed of. That's my purpose and goal.

Best Advice

Every difficult moment is a lesson learned. Growth doesn't come easy, it's a transition into something better. These are the moments that shape you, strengthen you, and build you into someone more resilient.

Listen to your gut. If something doesn't feel right, it usually isn't. Walking away is sometimes the bravest choice you can make.

All you need is that one person to believe in you to make you start believing in yourself. You can do anything you set your mind to.

It's okay to ask for help, it is not a weakness. Surround yourself with people who want to see you rise.

Success isn't shown by a full column or how busy you are. True success includes balance, boundaries, and time to breathe. Take a step back when needed.

And remember, the most important relationship is the one you have with yourself. Be kind to yourself. There is no such thing as perfect.

Confidence and happiness starts with you.

Strive to be the best version of yourself.

About Lucie McHugo

Lucie is the founder of The Beauty Room Birmingham. Her passion lies in advanced facial treatments and skin health, helping clients feel confident from the inside out. Known for her warm, empathetic approach, Lucie believes true skin confidence goes deeper than the surface.

Although she feels a few 'tweakments' can complement a good skincare routine, they are no substitute for long-term skin health. She loves to continually expand her knowledge, always exploring the latest treatments and techniques to deliver the best results. She is committed to CPD (Continuing Professional Development), continually learning and evolving.

Lucie believes in a holistic approach combining advanced facial treatments, active homecare products including skincare supplements, and lifestyle support to maximise results. Her mission is to help people glow with confidence and live their best life.

Salon Website: www.thebeautyroombirmingham.co.uk

Instagram: https://www.instagram.com/thebeautyroombirmingham

Facebook: www.facebook.com/thebeautyroombirmingham

lucie@thebeautyroombirmingham.co.uk

Salon Number 07931276413

From Receptionist to Leader: Lessons in Growth, Grit, and Generations

Amanda Basye

It was sometime in September 1980 when my mum, Kathleen, took me to see a vacant shop on the high street in Highgate Village. She had just qualified as a beauty therapist, a bold new direction for a working-class woman in her forties and had been tipped off about a unit becoming available. I was twelve, more interested in my Walkman than retail premises, but I remember the moment clearly. She looked through the glass, nodded, and said, "I think this could work."

Two months later, Hilltop opened its doors. And somehow, we've never looked back.

The early years were full of momentum. The salon grew quickly, from three treatment rooms to seven, and so did the steady flow of women through the doors. Highgate is the kind of village where relationships are everything. My mum understood that. Her hands were skilled, but it was her warmth and presence that brought people back.

By the age of 14, I was expected to help out. Every Saturday I'd cover reception, while my friends met up at the park or went into town. I hated missing out, but I showed up anyway, and I learned more than I realised. I learned how to manage a diary, calm a flustered client, make conversation with women I'd never otherwise meet. Without realising it, I was being trained, not in treatments, but in people.

If you're new to the industry, don't underestimate the power of reception. It's where you learn the heartbeat of the business, the flow, the language, the unspoken expectations.

Of course, I couldn't see the value at the time. I left school, trained as a shorthand secretary, and started working in the West End. I enjoyed the independence, the clothes, the commute, but deep down, I knew it wasn't where I was meant to be.

That clarity came at 23, when I had my first daughter, Vanessa. The pull to stay close to home was strong, so I started helping out at Hilltop again, just a few days a week on reception. It was a gentle return to something familiar, but something else was happening, too.

I was seeing the business differently.

From behind the desk, I watched the therapists work, really work, on more than just skin. I could see the change in clients as they returned each week: more open, more confident, more themselves. It was a quiet kind of transformation, and it fascinated me.

A few months later, I began my training to become a beauty therapist.

I was 25 with a toddler in tow, trying to learn facial muscles by day and negotiate with a two-year-old by night. The course was intense, but oddly, the toddler prepared me well. I loved the course, the way it blended structure with purpose, and the depth of knowledge behind the treatments. Understanding the science, especially anatomy and physiology, made the work feel serious and deeply satisfying. I soaked it all in and qualified two years later. Coming back to Hilltop as a therapist was seamless in some ways. I had a job, I knew the clients, I understood the pace. But it was also a test. I was the owner's daughter, and there was no room for special treatment.

And rightly so.

My parents had both come from nothing. They built their businesses with grit, humility, and a deep respect for hard work. There was no room for ego, only effort. I held myself to the same standard.

Whether you're new to the industry or decades in, the same principle applies: earn your place with actions, not assumptions. Respect is built when you show up consistently, without entitlement. Stay open. The learning never stops, and that's the beauty of it.

Soon, I had my own clients. I built relationships. I listened as women shared the parts of their lives that didn't fit neatly into small talk. And I started to understand the weight of what we offer in this industry, not just care, but connection. Not just treatment, but trust.

There's a quiet power in helping a woman feel like herself again. Not someone else. Not younger. Just... seen. And when that happens, something changes, in the way she carries herself, in her voice, in how she starts making choices that reflect who she really is.

The best therapists don't just treat skin, they hold space. That emotional skill is just as vital as technical expertise.

For 20 years, I worked side by side with my mum. We were close, and during those years, she was at her happiest. But in her late sixties, I started to notice small changes. A bit of confusion. Missed details. Repetition. Some days she was completely herself, which made me question what I was seeing. Then, one evening, she waited for the salon to empty, looked at me, and asked, "Am I going mad?"

My heart dropped. I'd done the research. I knew it was dementia.

I held her hand and told her she wasn't going mad, that her mind was just playing a few tricks. But we both knew the truth. The decision to step back had to be hers. She held on for as long as she could, but at the age of 77, she retired. It broke her heart, but her illness had made it impossible to continue.

What came next brought its own challenges. I'd imagined the transition would be hard, practically and emotionally, but I hadn't expected how complex things could become when grief, legacy, and ownership were involved.

These are the quiet battles that so many business owners face, especially in families. You carry on, even when it takes a toll in ways you didn't anticipate, because some things are worth standing up for.

And in the end, protecting Hilltop wasn't just about keeping it open. It was about honouring what my Mum built and choosing to build forward with intention.

Stepping into her shoes wasn't something I'd prepared for. I'd been a therapist, part of the team, not the leader. I had no formal business training. But I rolled up my sleeves and got to work. The early days were messy. I'd gone on to have another daughter, Hannah, and she was still so young when everything began to shift. The team needed guidance. My mum was in the grips of dementia. And I was trying to hold it all, the business, my family, the emotional weight of watching someone you love slowly change. Looking back now, it was survival mode.

And here's the truth no one says often enough: women are expected to hold everything together, the home, the team, the people they love, often without ever being asked how they're doing. But if you're balancing any of it, in any way, don't overlook the strength in that. It might not always feel graceful, but it's powerful.

We're not here to be perfect, just present. And if you're still showing up, even on the hard days, that's more than enough.

What kept me going was knowing that Hilltop mattered. Not just to me, but to the community we'd served for decades. It had become a place of trust, of consistency, of care. That legacy couldn't be lost.

Over time, the team adjusted. Respect built quietly. And the business evolved.

Both of my daughters, Vanessa and Hannah, started out the same way I did, working Saturdays on reception, before stepping away to explore other careers. They've each returned with new perspectives and skills, and today, Hilltop is shaped by their presence as much as mine. We're not just a family business, we're a business built by family

Now, the next generation is beginning to find her feet. My granddaughter, Vanessa's eldest, has started helping out at reception. She's in sixth form, focused on her own future, but she's chosen to spend time here. Not because we've nudged her toward the business, but because she recognises that mastering the salon phone is practically a survival skill.

The way she carries herself has already begun to shift. There's something valuable in showing up, being around people, and holding your own in a professional space, skills that will serve her well in whatever she chooses to do next.

Mum passed away not long ago. Her illness meant she never saw the full picture of what we've built. But I like to think she's watching now, from somewhere just out of sight, proud, peaceful, and quietly smiling.

She started Hilltop with a treatment couch, a reception desk, and a dream. And somehow, all these years later, we're still here, proof that beauty, when grounded in purpose, never really fades.

There's no single path in this industry, and that's what makes it meaningful. Some arrive early, others return later, but the work will always welcome you. If you lead with care, stay curious, and keep taking small steps, your impact will grow, often when you least expect it. That's what real leadership looks like.

What I've Learned Along the Way

- You don't have to be loud to be impactful. There's strength in quiet confidence, in showing up steadily and letting your work speak for itself.
- Leadership doesn't arrive all at once. It builds in the background, through choices, conversations, and a thousand quiet moments when you simply kept going.
- Being a therapist is never just about the treatment. It's about trust. Clients return not just because of how their skin looks, but how they feel in your company.
- You can love the work and still feel tired. That doesn't make you any less dedicated, just human.
- If you're holding a lot, family, business, grief, growth, please know that you're not alone. You don't have to carry it all perfectly.
- Stay open. The best therapists (and leaders) are the ones who keep learning, even when they've been doing it for decades.
- And when you doubt yourself, which you will, at some point, come back to your values. Your why. The quieter voice inside that says, this matters.

About Amanda Basye

Amanda Basye is the owner of Hilltop Advanced Skin & Beauty, a skin and laser clinic in Highgate Village, North London. With over 30 years of experience as a beauty therapist, she works with care, connection, and quiet strength.

As the second generation at the helm of her family's business, Amanda now runs Hilltop alongside her daughters, Vanessa and Hannah, continuing a legacy that began in 1980. Hilltop has long remained a trusted destination for skin health and personalised care.

Amanda's wider studies in spiritual counselling, breathwork facilitation, and nutrition bring a deeper dimension to her work, blending the clinical with the intuitive, and the technical with the human.

She is passionate about helping people feel at home in their skin, and about guiding the next generation of therapists to grow with confidence, curiosity, and heart.

Website: www.hilltopbeautysalon.com

Instagram: https://www.instagram.com/hilltopbeautysalon/

Facebook: https://www.facebook.com/hilltopbeautysalon/

LinkedIn: www.linkedin.com/in/amanda-basye-8123baa2

From Set Back To Skin Success

Lauren Gill

I have wanted to be a beauty therapist for as long as I can remember. As a child, I would play a game with my mum where I'd dash upstairs, change into my 'uniform,' pack a little kit bag, and wait beside her mobile phone. She'd call from the house landline pretending to book an appointment, and I'd walk downstairs, knock on the door, and greet her like a real client. I called my imaginary business Super Salon. I even had laminated price lists – and probably made a few pounds each week. If only I'd known then that those childhood dreams would one day become a reality.

At sixteen, I left school still chasing that same dream. I qualified with my NVQ Levels 2 and 3 and leapt straight into my first job in a local salon. It gave me a grounding in professional treatment standards and salon life, but I quickly realised that my passion leaned more toward facials, skincare, and the calm, immersive atmosphere of massage. I moved to a beautiful spa in the Cotswolds, a luxury environment that helped me refine my skills. Over the next few years, I progressed from spa therapist to spa manager. But while the setting was stunning, the role became predictable. I craved something more – ssomething with pace, variety, challenge. I was itching to push myself.

So, I did what felt right – and terrifying.

I joined Steiner as a Facialist, packed up my life, and set sail. Working on cruise ships allowed me to travel the world and meet people from every background imaginable.

Life on board was fast-paced, competitive, and incredibly structured. You had to be adaptable, polished, and professional at all times. It was here that I truly honed my customer service skills – learning how to read a client, manage expectations, and communicate with warmth and confidence. But more than anything, it was where I learned how to deliver exceptional client care. No two days were the same, and I thrived on the energy and challenge.

It was in the MediSpa on board that I met Dr. Freitas – someone who saw something in me that I hadn't fully owned yet. He recognised how much I cared about results, how deeply I wanted to understand skin and deliver more than just a relaxing experience. He told me I had more to give – and I believed him.

When I returned to dry land, I followed that instinct. I found a job in a skin clinic – and felt instantly at home. Knowing I wanted to specialise further I enrolled in my CIBTAC Level 4 and soaked up everything I could: advanced skin science, microneedling, chemical peeling, investigative consultations.

My CIBTAC Level 4 was a game changer.

While I'd had lots of brand and manufacturer training and felt confident performing skin treatments, I soon realised how little I actually knew. I understood the basics, but this course took a deep dive into the science of skin. I learned how treatments stimulate different responses, how ingredients interact with various cells, and how to apply this knowledge in real-time.

What I knew before wasn't worth knowing in comparison. I came out the other side more confident, more capable, and more passionate than ever. I officially became a skin geek!

I genuinely loved my job. It all made sense. I wasn't just doing treatments anymore. I was transforming skin. I had a full diary, wonderful clients, and was thriving professionally.

Then came March 2020...

When the first national lockdown hit, and I was furloughed like so many other therapists, I stayed optimistic. I kept in close contact with the clinic owner, and it felt like this was just an extended break. We all assumed it would be full steam ahead when we reopened.

But in May 2020, just after my 27th birthday, I received a phone call that changed everything.

I was being made redundant.

At first, I was numb. I had invested so much – my time, my energy, my heart – into that job. I was passionate about the treatments, about educating clients, and about seeing real skin results. To lose it all without warning, in the middle of a global crisis, felt like the rug had been pulled from under me. The financial fear was one thing – but the emotional impact was harder.

I didn't just lose a job. I lost a sense of identity, of purpose.

I gave myself a few days to absorb it, but soon after, something unexpected started to happen – I began receiving messages from clients. They were checking in, asking where I would be working next, and expressing how much they were looking forward to rebooking once restrictions lifted. It was their words – their belief in me – that planted the first seed.

At first, I assumed I'd need to find another clinic. But the reality was — no one was hiring. Most places weren't even open. However, I had my experience, my education, and my love for tailoring every facial to each client's skin.

The more I thought about it, the more I questioned whether I wanted to work someone else's protocols again. I had a clear vision of how I liked to treat skin. I wanted flexibility, freedom, and a strong ethical focus. Could I do this on my own? What did I honestly have to lose?

I started researching. It was just an idea at first – a whisper of a "what if." I was saving for a house at the time and had an income from working shifts at COVID vaccination centres. I drafted a business plan, crunched numbers, spoke to suppliers. I knew exactly which brands and machines I believed in. I sourced the technology that aligned with my ethos: results-driven, ethical, and effective. I reached out to a local clinic that was open to renting me space for a couple of days a week. It was all falling into place.

By the end of June, I was ready.

But before I could open the doors, my world changed again. In July, just two months after losing my job, my brother Matthew* lost his long battle with mental health. I was devastated. There are no words to fully describe that kind of loss. He was my big brother – always proud, always supportive. Grieving him while trying to keep moving forward felt impossible. But in the middle of that pain, I knew I had to hold onto something. Starting the business wasn't just about my career anymore. It became a lifeline. A way to pour my energy into something that felt hopeful when everything else felt broken.

Matthew had always been supportive of me. He'd often tell people how proud he was of what I was achieving in my career.

This became more than a business – it became a promise. To honour him. To keep going.

The ever-changing government guidance for the beauty and aesthetics industry didn't help. Dates kept shifting, and it wasn't until mid-August that I was finally allowed to begin working – and even then, only offering non-contact services. No hands-on facials – just non-contact sessions and conversations from a distance. But clients still came. They booked LED not just for the benefits, but because they believed in me. I'll never forget that feeling. It was humbling, emotional, and deeply motivating.

In honour of my brother and everything he believed in me for, I pressed on. Lauren Gill Skin Specialist was never part of the plan – it was my response to loss, built on courage and care. I quietly promised I'd make him, and myself, proud.

Once the doors were open properly, things began to move quickly. I continued to invest in equipment and brands that aligned with my ethos – results-led, ethical, and backed by science. Within four months, I had outgrown the two-day rental room and made the leap to a larger space of my own.

It was both exhilarating and terrifying. I was still only a few months into running my own business, juggling everything from stock control to social media, treatment planning to tax returns. But the response was incredible – every new client has come through word of mouth, referrals, or someone stumbling across my story. The diary has remained busy. The business has matured. And I've never lost sight of why I started.

Clients often told me they came to me because I took the time to explain things, to educate without overwhelm, and to personalise every plan. That's always been my focus: to deliver honest, ethical skincare that gives real results and empowers people to understand their own skin.

It's the little things that clients remember. They may arrive flustered and drop their belongings wherever they land. During treatment, I'll take a moment to gently fold or hang their clothing, place their jewellery on a tray, and tidy their things. After the treatment they feel cared for.

It shows them that I notice the small details – and that I do truly care about their treatment experience.

I always offer refreshments before and after treatment and take a seat with each client to review their goals. I remind them of what we're doing and why, invite any questions, and allow time to talk through changes since their last visit. I never want clients to feel rushed – I build in 15 minutes extra for every appointment just to ensure we have time to connect.

I'm passionate about what I do, and I let my clients see that excitement. I talk openly with them about their skin, their progress, and the next steps. Over time, it's created trust. Many no longer book treatments from a menu – they simply show up and hand over their skin to me. That trust is something I never take for granted.

Even while running the clinic solo, I've never stopped learning. I attend Professional Beauty London each year to stay current with new innovations and technology. I'm a proud member of the Beauty Directors Club and always stay connected to like-minded professionals in the industry. Every decision I've made – comes back to one core goal: to empower clients with skin confidence through science, integrity, and the upmost care.

Lauren Gill Skin Specialist may have begun in the shadows of uncertainty and grief, but it has grown into something I'm incredibly proud of.

From "Super Salon" as a child to international spas, from

redundancy to resilience, from grief to growth – every chapter has shaped the therapist and businesswoman I've become. This journey has been built with equal parts pain and purpose, and I'm proud of what I've created.

And this? This is just the beginning.

*For Matthew — who always believed in me

About Lauren Gill

Lauren is the founder of Lauren Gill Skin Specialist, an advanced skin clinic built on passion, precision, and personal resilience. Starting her career at sixteen, she gained experience across salons, spas, and cruise ships, eventually progressing to clinic management. Her passion for skin health led her to specialise in aesthetics, achieving her CIBTAC Level 4 with distinctions in multiple disciplines.

In 2020, Lauren launched Lauren Gill Skin Specialist with the goal of delivering ethical, evidence-based treatments tailored to each client's needs. Her clinic has since grown steadily through word of mouth and a reputation for integrity, education, and visible results. Lauren continues to invest in the latest technology and training to stay at the forefront of the industry, offering a wide range of advanced treatments including IPL, fractional laser, micro-needling, mesotherapy, and skin peels. Her focus remains on delivering high standards of care and helping clients achieve long-term skin confidence.

www.lgskinspecialist.co.uk

www.instagram.com/lg_skinspecialist

https://www.facebook.com/lgskinspecialist/

Little Miss Dyslexia: A Hustler With Heart

Samantha Harrop

This is going to sound like the beginning of an American film ... It starts with my sisters and me. We were still in primary school, crossing the railway bridge to reach a little orchard where we'd scrump plums to sell – 2p and 3p depending on the size. I mean, this was the 1980s, and you could get three sweets for half a penny from the sweet van that came once a week.

We did land ourselves in trouble a few times, like when my middle sister got stuck in a tree. I remember running home while she was still hanging there and our little sister stayed behind, upset that I couldn't take her with me. But she would've slowed me down, and I was terrified there was going to be a fall. I ran as fast as I could, knocked on our neighbour's door, and asked her to help. I prayed – first, that she could help... and second, that she wouldn't tell our mum what we'd been up to.

Being the eldest of three, I felt responsible for my sisters – although I didn't fully understand what that meant until fear hit me. That fear and uncertainty?

It's a familiar feeling when you run your own business.

Once we had enough fruit, we'd wash it in a friend's bath and then sell it at the park. We then had the money to buy two stick lollipops, break them in half, and resell them to make a profit. Honestly, we were proper little hustlers – entrepreneurial, without even knowing it.

At Christmas, we'd go carol singing. I was already delegating, one of our cousins had the voice of an angel, and my youngest sister, with her shy smile, blonde hair, and blue eyes, melted hearts. They were the perfect duo. We'd split the money at the end. But I'm getting ahead of myself because before that was Guy Fawkes Night. Another opportunity. I'd ask my grandad for old clothes, stuff them with newspaper, pop my "Guy" in a wheelbarrow, and go knocking at doors: "Penny for the Guy!"

Honestly, I have so many stories. My aunt helped me set up a Better Wear catalog round. I think I was around 12 at the time. I really smile now, thinking of that little girl trying her hardest, thinking outside the box, doing so well… all while believing she wasn't good enough. That she was stupid. That she was slow. That she'd never become much – because she was dyslexic.

I grew up embarrassed, scared, riddled with shame. I hated being different. I was teased, humiliated, so I learned early to hide behind humour. I became the funny out going one, anything but the "stupid dyslexic" one. My middle sister was the clever one, the youngest was the pretty one, and even though I had changed my label, I still believed I was the stupid one.

At 15, I took my first bold step into the real world and left school. I'd already been working Saturdays at a high-end hair salon, and I began a three-year apprenticeship. I was also babysitting and working as a washer-upper first at a hotel (until they realised I was underage), then at a local pub.

Hairdressing was a big leap forward.

But I was also told, "That's all you're good for – you don't need brains to be a hairdresser." Despite that, I absolutely loved the salon. I was around older, worldly people, always learning, and let me tell you, you need so many incredible skills being a hairdresser and that training was integral to the woman I'd become.

Fast forward to my late twenties. I felt at a crossroads and decided to go back to college to learn nails, I thought it would complement my hairdressing. Nails were just taking off, and my uncle, who spent a lot of time in the States, encouraged me to pursue it. But as luck would have it, I was interviewed by an old salon client who saw potential in me – not just as a nail tech, (let me just explain myself, no one is JUST anything I mean more training required than just nails) but as a beautician. I signed up for the full-time course as a mature student at 28.

At the same time, I set up a spray tanning business with a college friend. We'd go to people's houses - we called them "Footballers' Wives" parties. They were great fun, and soon we earned enough to buy another machine and split the business so we could earn more individually.

Qualifying was hard. I had notes pinned all over my house to memorise the anatomy. I made up songs to remember sequences. Still embarrassed about my dyslexia, I didn't want to ask for help. So when I passed – I cried with relief and pride. That girl, once riddled with shame, had done it. She actually did it, it felt huge, I had defied the "stupid" label. I was feeling unstoppable, for the first time I had belief in myself and my own capabilities that monkey on my back was being quietened

My first role as a beautician was at Saks. The salon training and time with the team were amazing, and the Saks Awards were unforgettable. Still unable to sit still, I launched another venture

– a mobile pamper party business with a colleague. We'd go to people's homes, offering treatments for groups of four or more. We had a rule: whoever got the party host could share their details with the guests. It worked brilliantly as we built our home-based clienteles. Eventually, we couldn't fit in any more bookings between our salon work and our growing mobile businesses. Around this time, I wound down my hairdressing clients and pointed them in a new direction.

Today, I run my business from a tranquil, purpose-built cabin, a beautiful skin retreat in my garden. I was so busy with mobile clients that I took the plunge and left Saks. I'd had wonderful years working for the company and I'm still in contact with friends I made to this day, but it was time to move on and start what I had been working towards all along, my own business. The cabin was built because I simply couldn't get to everyone's homes anymore. I'm so grateful to say that I still have clients that have been with me for over 20 years.

My reputation brings clients from far and wide, all mainly from word of mouth.

I absolutely love my work and the genuine connections I've made. By showing up every day as myself, I've created something real. My advice? Don't try to copy anyone else. Sit in your space. Own it. You, the fabulous human reading this - you are unique. You have a special, nurturing power. Grow your own kind of clientele - because that's who you'll spend most of your time with.

My business has evolved - just like we do. It would be strange if it didn't. I used to have a treatment menu a mile long… nails, spray tans, massages, detoxification, bamboo, hot stones, lava shells, Tibetan bundles, aromatherapy, facials, more facials, waxing, lashes, Minx, Bio Sculpture - you name it.

But that wasn't me. I was trying too hard to offer everything, (people pleasers please stand up) it pulled me away from what I loved most.

During college, I fell in love with skin – facials brought me pure joy. That's why I decided to stay on and further educate myself. Ironically, I didn't even enjoy doing nails, the very reason I'd enrolled in the first place. But the universe had other plans. That chance encounter changed everything. I could do a whole other chapter on putting out to the universe, if you haven't read The Secret I highly recommend it, it's life changing

It took burnout and a mentor to wake me up. I now only offer facial treatments. My menu is packed with incredible facial equipment paired with my holistic approach. Everything is bespoke, not just down to the skin wants and needs but how that client is doing in oneself, I have continued to be educated in new techniques, my intuition from continued years, of hands on, and new learnings after spending huge amounts of hours being taught how to be a life coach, ending with my certification in Bali, has helped me to give a more complete holistic approach to every client's individual needs.

Lockdown was also a turning point. It gave us space between clients – space I've continued. My clients love arriving to a warm smile and leaving to a warm wave. No interruptions. No phones. No knocks at the door. Just birdsong and rain on the roof. Pure luxury, from start to finish.

Here's what I've learned: Ask for help, I know it can be a hard thing to do, but the right people want to help you and see you succeed. Find a mentor. My business transformed when I found the perfect mentor.

When Susan had me break down my finances, I was shocked. I cried, really cried. How had I worked so hard and still got it so wrong? I considered giving it all up... but when I asked myself, "Do I really want to close my doors?" The answer was a definite no! So changes had to be put into place so that I could have a healthy business.

Running a business isn't just about your clients though I wish it were. Spending time with beautiful people, changing lives, hearing their stories – it's a privilege. But we still need to earn a living. When your work feels good and you're a natural giving and nurturing person . . . sometimes, it doesn't feel like work. And we forget to charge.

So, know your numbers. Work out your pricing. Understand exactly what each treatment costs you.

Remember when you're working as a solo operator, you need to factor your holidays, and hopefully not many sick days, so when you see money in the bank hold back before you spend it. Ummm not like me! I've learnt the hard way, any extra money in the bank meant I could add new equipment, I'm not saying don't add to your repertoire, but it's easy to forget you might have a quieter month due to holidays and you may find yourself with a very low wage one month

Mistakes help you grow. And if ever you feel uncertain, ask yourself - then reach out. I remember getting anxiety back at Saks if a certain client was booked in. We've all had them. But when you work for yourself, you can decide who fits. You're allowed to say no. You deserve to enjoy your work.

Cut yourself some slack. Appreciate how far you've come. Be brave.

It might have taken me until the third Beauty and the Best book to say YES... but I said it.

And now? I'm enjoying the process.

I'm so grateful to share this experience - with you, and with the beautiful, inspiring people on these pages.

Dyslexia once felt like my biggest weakness, but I actually see it now as my greatest strength. Who would have thought, that little girl would end up running her own business, but then again maybe, the writing really was up a tree all along, and I just had to climb it!

Big love always, Sam xx

About Samantha Harrop

Samantha Harrop has over 20 years of experience in the beauty industry, she is a trusted and sought-after facialist known for her exceptional results, combining a unique blend of advanced technology and holistic hands-on techniques, working from her home based clinic. Samantha welcomes clients from near and far, offering deeply personalised treatments tailored to each individual's needs and desires.

Samantha's approach is both intuitive and informed, always grounded in continuous learning and professional development. Her passion for skincare and client care is matched by her commitment to the next generation of beauty professionals. She has spoken with pride, care and honesty at Professional Beauty up and down the country and enjoys mentoring newcomers and old in the industry.

Warm, dedicated and always evolving. Samantha brings heart and expertise to every treatment she performs.

Website - https://www.samanthaharropskincare.co.uk/

Facebook - https://www.facebook.com/samhskinandbeauty

Instagram - https://www.instagram.com/samhskinandbeauty/

Email - sam.harrop@icloud.com

Manage Your Way!

Anastasia Korabukhina

Every journey begins with a single decision, and mine was to embrace change and create a life that reflected my values. This is the story of how I transitioned from law to the beauty industry, built a thriving business, and discovered the power of leading with purpose.

Growing up in Murmansk, a city surrounded by the beauty of the Arctic, I completed my schooling in an environment that taught me resilience and adaptability. My parents, both highly educated, instilled in me the importance of respect, understanding, and the belief that education is the foundation of a meaningful life. These values became the cornerstone of my personal and professional journey.

After finishing school, I pursued a law degree at the prestigious Saint Petersburg State University. It was a challenging yet rewarding experience that laid the foundation for my professional growth. However, my ambitions didn't stop there. I decided to broaden my horizons and moved to London to pursue a master's degree. It was during this time that I made a life-changing decision: to retrain as a lawyer in the United Kingdom. This decision was not just about adapting to a new legal system but about embracing a new culture and way of life.

However, life had other plans. At 27, I became pregnant, and this pivotal moment inspired me to explore a new path — opening a hair and beauty salon. The idea was sparked by a suggestion from a friend, and while I had always been intrigued by the idea of running my own business, I had never taken the leap. This was my chance.

The journey to opening my salon was anything but straightforward. My friend, who initially proposed the idea, decided not to continue, leaving me to take the reins. At six months pregnant, I found myself negotiating leases, organising the opening, and handling every detail. It was a whirlwind, but in hindsight, it was the perfect time. On October 3rd, 2011, I opened the doors to my salon, which has now been thriving for nearly 14 years.

Located in a neighbourhood I knew well, I saw an untapped niche — a demand for high-quality services among local residents who valued convenience and excellence. The space we found was perfect, with large windows overlooking the water, creating a serene and relaxing atmosphere for both clients and staff. Over the years, we've built a loyal client base and fostered warm relationships with neighbouring businesses and communities. This sense of connection and collaboration has been one of the most rewarding aspects of running the salon.

The salon became more than just a business. It became a reflection of my values and vision. I wanted to build a space that prioritised respect, care, excellence and attention to detail, not just for clients but for staff as well. These principles guided every decision, from the services we offered to the atmosphere we created.

But the journey hasn't been without its challenges. As someone who transitioned from law to the hair and beauty industry,

I faced skepticism and doubt. People questioned my knowledge and experience, and I had to learn everything from scratch. There were no templates or mentors to guide me. I relied on my intuition and high standards to build the business. Slowly but surely, I adapted, evolved, and created a microcosm that reflects my values and vision.

Resilience became my greatest ally. There were moments when I felt overwhelmed, especially in the early days when I was juggling a new business and motherhood. I remember days when I would work late into the night, balancing the demands of running a business with the responsibilities of being a new mother. But I came to understand that challenges are opportunities to grow. Every setback taught me something new, whether it was about managing people, improving services, or adapting to change.

Listening also became a cornerstone of my approach. Whether it's clients, staff, or my own instincts, listening has been the foundation of trust and growth. I've found that when you truly hear people, you can create meaningful connections and build loyalty. This applies not just in business but in every aspect of life.

Leading by example has been another key to my success. As a business owner, your actions set the tone for your team. By demonstrating respect, care, and a commitment to excellence, you inspire others to do the same. This creates a positive and supportive environment where everyone can thrive. I've always believed that a salon is more than just a place for services — it's a space for connection, energy exchange, and personal transformation.

Above all, staying true to my values has been the most important lesson. In a world that often prioritises quick wins and shortcuts, holding onto your principles can be challenging. But it's also what sets you apart.

For me, respect, care, and excellence are not just words – they are the foundation of everything I do. They guide my decisions, shape my relationships, and define my success.

What has truly defined my approach is the way I've built trust and meaningful relationships with both clients and staff. Clients often tell me they feel heard and understood, and that they are treated as individuals, not just customers. This feedback has been a cornerstone of my business philosophy. I've always believed that creating a feel-good experience is about more than just the services we provide – it's about fostering trust, comfort, and a sense of belonging. This approach has not only built long-term loyalty but has also encouraged word-of-mouth referrals, which have been instrumental in our growth.

My team plays a vital role in this success. I've worked hard to create a positive and respectful work culture where staff feel valued and supported. By recognising their strengths and weaknesses, giving them freedom and respect, and mentoring them around the salon's core values, I've built a team that shares my vision. Staff often describe the salon as a calm and welcoming environment, a place where they can thrive both professionally and personally. This alignment of values has created a strong sense of chemistry and collaboration within the team, which clients can feel the moment they walk through the door.

As a business owner, I've also embraced the importance of accountability. I hold myself responsible for the results we achieve, the people we serve, and the mission we uphold. This mindset has helped me navigate challenges with resilience and a problem-solving attitude. Whether it's addressing client feedback, improving hygiene standards, or introducing innovative services, I've always prioritised continuous improvement. This commitment to growth has been key to maintaining high standards and staying ahead in a competitive industry.

My message to anyone reading this is simple: success is not about following a predefined path but about creating your own. It's about staying true to your values, embracing change, and leading with purpose. Whether you're in the beauty industry or another field, the principles of respect, care, and excellence are universal. They are the keys to building trust, fostering loyalty, and achieving meaningful success.

Today, I balance my role as a salon owner with my work in an international law firm. This unique combination allows me to bring diverse perspectives to both fields. I'm also a proud wife and mother of my children. My life is a blend of family, business, and professional growth, and I wouldn't have it any other way.

Through this journey, I've learned that success is not about following a predefined path but about creating your own. It's about embracing change, learning from challenges, and staying true to your values. To anyone considering a leap into the unknown, I say this: trust your instincts, be resilient, and manage your way.

About Anastasia Korabukhina

Anastasia Korabukhina is a dynamic entrepreneur and legal professional with a unique journey spanning two industries. Born in Russia, she retrained as a lawyer in the UK and later founded a thriving hair and beauty salon in London.

With nearly 14 years of experience in the beauty industry, Anastasia combines her legal expertise with her passion for business. She is dedicated to creating a welcoming and transformative experience for her clients, fostering a positive and respectful work culture, and mentoring other business owners in the industry. Anastasia lives in London with her husband, children, and her younger sister.

https://www.linkedin.com/in/anastasiakorabukhina

https://www.instagram.com/anastasia_korabukhina

anastasia.korabukhina@gmail.com

https://www.va-salon.com

https://www.instagram.com/vasalonlondon

https://www.facebook.com/vasalonlondon

It's Never Too Late, If It's What You Really Want To Do!

Jane Mary Lunn

I had been interested in Beauty since the age of 20, but I guess, due to a lack of confidence in myself, I never pursued it. I was far too easily swayed by other people's opinions back then and this led me down a totally different path. I didn't know then but because I didn't have that solid foundation growing up, I lacked the necessary skills and confidence to follow my heart. My Mum was forced to marry my dad due to her first sexual encounter resulting in her becoming pregnant with me, but an incident with him caused her to flee and give birth to me elsewhere. Then when I was aged 4/5, she left for Switzerland to work for the WHO. I felt so abandoned. I didn't know who my dad was and now my mum had left me too. My Nan and Grandad did their best, but it was a very unhappy time for me growing up without my mum, and even more so, living with an auntie (8yrs older than me) that had a strained relationship with her own mum, that for her to see her mum care for her little niece so lovingly, she understandably became jealous and then took that jealousy out in me.

I remember during Covid when Susan asked the ladies in the BDC to contribute to her first BATB book and I immediately thought I would love to do that! However, as the stories came in to read, it made me reflect on my own childhood and other things that happened too that I had pushed far back into my subconscious that I couldn't possibly share with anyone else. I hadn't even told my hubby of nearly 30 years, let alone think about sharing these events with anyone else.

What this prompted for me though during this time was to begin my journey of healing. I very soon began training to become a Life and Health Coach with the Health Coach Institute in the US, which I quickly came to realise that, even though I embarked on this training to help others, it did actually really help me heal myself from the traumas of my past.

Even though these traumas have held me back to some extent, they have also shaped who I am today. They led me to help others, something I really love to do. Instead of me addressing my own traumas, I instinctively focussed on asking others about their lives thus protecting myself as I didn't want anyone asking me about mine. Even so, helping others gives me great joy, it makes me happy. That's why I loved teaching, until it became so untenable I couldn't continue. I think that's why I love the feeling I get at the salon and now even more so that I am providing treatments. I would never have thought that performing such a service for someone could bring so much joy. Especially now when people are becoming much more detached and disconnected on a personal level, it is such a privilege and pleasure to be in an industry whereby that real human connection is so prevalent.

I didn't initially train fully in beauty when I bought Estetica. I just did the odd CPD course here and there. I had done so much studying to become a teacher I was so over any further studying at the time. Plus, I felt I didn't really need to as I inherited staff to do all the treatments we offered anyway and I could just focus on the management side of it.

Looking back now though, I believe it would have been much wiser if I had done. I have found that it is all too easy for staff to pull the wool over your eyes if you're not trained in the industry you're in, and you don't really know what they are doing. You don't know how a beauty salon should be run successfully, effectively and efficiently.

So, if you are thinking of buying a beauty business or if you already have one but aren't beauty trained, go and get yourself trained up. Even if you think it is too late to retrain, or that you think you aren't even going to do the treatments on clients anyway, or you have qualifications far greater than a level 2 or 3, go and get yourself trained up. You obviously have some interest in the beauty industry if you're thinking of buying a beauty business or you have one already but aren't beauty trained. As Nike says 'Just Do It'. Take control over your business and direct it where you want it to go. It will stand you in a much better position if you do.

After the difficulties that Covid brought for many health and beauty businesses, I finally thought I had found a staff member who was genuine, professional and caring, and someone I could hand over my business to in the future. She was well qualified, determined and passionate about her career and most importantly she cared about our clients.

Well, that is what I believed at the start anyway!

There were a few issues I had but nothing I thought couldn't be sorted. However, after two years, I eventually found out what she was really like and it ended up becoming an utter nightmare. She had been seeing clients out of hours, getting them to pay her directly. She stole cash from the till, she defrauded clients and later flooded the entire building! Not only did I allow this person to nearly ruin my business but also my sanity too.

However, after many sleepless nights, feelings of helplessness and hopelessness with many unanswered questions, I am so thankful to have survived this and come out the other side. Plus, if I had never experienced this, I would never have had to step in to continue with our clients' CACI courses. I would never have known the sheer joy I am experiencing now. Who would have thought that such a disastrous experience could result in something so very special for me. You just never know what's around the corner! So never give up when things do not go your way or if you ever think you cannot take anymore, just keep going and there will be a silver lining.

Yes, I had a difficult start in life but it doesn't mean that it always has to be that way, and if you've had a difficult upbringing, I want to tell you that, you can find happiness too. It may have taken me some time and even though I have had lots of happy moments during my lifetime, I have recently found something truly wonderful whilst performing my CACI facials. It has become such a pleasure, welcoming clients into the salon and using the magic of CACI on them, seeing their results develop and seeing how happy it makes them too. It brings me so much joy to see this that I cannot wait to develop my skills further. Obviously, at the grand old age of 58, there will only be so far I can go but I want to excel in the area of skincare and facials as much as I can. I want to be able to offer a wide range of treatments to help a wide range of concerns for my clients. I have also been using my coaching skills alongside my CACI facials and 'continued to coach on a one to one basis, part time. It has all been working extremely well so far.

My words of guidance to others that have had trauma or are still struggling with past trauma is to set some time aside for yourself, find a quiet place and seek what it is that YOU truly want in life then imagine you already have it.

Then step into your future happy successful self and ask yourself: *How do you feel? Have a good look around. What do you see? What are you wearing? How are others looking at you?*

Really get to experience your future, happy, successful self and go after her.

Get to really know what you want, find the courage to go after your dream, the confidence will come later, keep going, keep looking for solutions.

Even though I have experienced many bumps along my life journey, I have kept going, sometimes extremely slowly, but none the less, I have kept going. Through my many challenges in life and in business during these recent times, I felt at times I wanted to throw the towel in and give it all up but I am so glad I didn't as I am enjoying my salon life more now than I ever have before.

So, thank you so much for all those experiences and challenges for leading me to my best life right now.

About Jane Mary Lunn

After a traumatic start in life, Jane found strength through her faith in God and love of sport, which helped her navigate early challenges. Despite starting on the wrong foot, she's always wanted to be happy and pursued happiness throughout her life, even through setbacks. Jane worked in various jobs before discovering her "happy place" in teaching. But after 12 years, the joy faded – buried under relentless demands and a lack of appreciation.

Determined to find a better work-life balance, she discovered a well-established beauty salon in West Yorkshire – and is now the owner of an award-winning salon in the village of Lindley. Jane is an Advanced CACI Therapist and a certified Transformational Life and Health Coach. She helps women overcome their life's challenges to create the calm, balanced, happy life they long for.

Jane is also a Collagen Lift Therapist and recently completed her VTCT Level 3 in Facials and Skincare. She is now pursuing further study in Level 4 and beyond.

Website: www.esteticabeautyclinic.co.uk

Instagram – esteticabeautyclinic

Facebook Estetica beauty Lindley

Email for Estetica:

esteticabeautyclinic@live.co,uk

Email for coaching: janemarylunn@live.co.uk

Durham To Bahrain And Back

Rachael Howard

If I had passed my nursing exam at 18, I probably wouldn't be writing this today.

Most of the women in my family were either nurses or teachers—that was the expected path. Steady, respectable careers. And while I respected the work, something inside me always whispered, "Is that really all there is?"

A Restless Start

After school, I ended up in a traditional office role. It didn't take long before the routine began to wear on me. The conversations were always the same—gardening, pensions, early retirement. And eventually, you'd hear that someone had passed away. It felt like life was passing by in slow motion, without passion or purpose.

Something inside me knew: there has to be more to life than this.

A Serendipitous Discovery

Then one day, by complete chance—or maybe something deeper—I stumbled across a leaflet advertising an introductory course at Darlington college. It offered evening classes in aromatherapy, reflexology, and body massage. I wasn't even sure what half of those things really meant at the time, but something about it intrigued me.

I visited the college, spoke to the lecturer, and signed up on the spot. There were just ten of us in the class—nine of them were nurses. I instantly felt at home. From the very first session, I was hooked.

Following The Spark

What began as a curiosity quickly turned into a passion. I completed a year in body massage, then another in aromatherapy. The deeper I went, the more I realised this was what I was meant to do. It wasn't just about helping others relax – it was about caring, healing, and connection.

Eventually, I left my full-time office job to study for a BTEC ND in beauty therapy at Gateshead College. It was a leap of faith, but one that felt right.

From Durham To The Open Sea

With some hands-on salon experience under my belt, I decided to go even further—I applied for a role as a beauty therapist on cruise ships with Steiner. When I received the job offer, I was beyond thrilled. It was an opportunity to combine my love for beauty therapy with a desire to travel and explore.

Working on board those ships was exhilarating. I served on two very different vessels, each with its own clientele and culture. But my mission remained the same: to help people pause, reset, and feel better about themselves.

Turning Point

After my contract ended, I considered staying on. One of the ships was heading to Alaska next, and looking back, I do wish I had stayed. But instead, I returned to back Durham briefly and began working in spas around the country – Stratford-upon-Avon, Leeds, and beyond.

No matter where I went, I noticed something: I loved teaching my clients. I enjoyed explaining skincare, wellness, and how to care for their bodies. That joy sparked a new idea: What if I became a teacher?

The Teacher I Never Expected To Be

It's funny—if someone had told me in school that I'd one day become a teacher, I would've laughed and said, "Not a chance." But I couldn't deny how fulfilled I felt helping others learn.

I earned my teaching qualification and assessor's award and began teaching part-time in the North East. But I wanted more – I wanted to teach full-time, to fully immerse myself in that world.

Then came an opportunity that would change my life forever: a teaching position in Bahrain.

Bahrain: A Life-Changing Experience

After several phone calls, interviews, and even some old-fashioned faxes (yes, faxes!), I got the job. Only then did I look up where Bahrain was—just across the causeway from Saudi Arabia!

Moving there was a leap, but one I'll never regret. The students I taught—mostly young women—were warm, generous, and eager to learn. Some came from very modest backgrounds, yet they arrived in class with trays of homemade samosas and endless enthusiasm. I had a full time teaching schedule six days a week. Found myself teaching ITEC Beauty Therapy government funded students during the daytime and Holistic Therapies to ex pat fee paying students on an evening.

Teaching them wasn't just about beauty techniques. It was about empowerment. It was about showing them their worth, their potential. I felt so lucky to be part of their journey.

Saying Goodbye

Sadly, after three incredible years, my contract ended due to Government funding and cultural issues for women working in Bahrain. I relocated to the North West of the UK and took a role in spa management , but I quickly realised I missed the hands-on connection with people. I missed the teaching, the purpose.

Not long after, I was offered a role as an educator for a highly acclaimed and award winning cosmeceutical skincare brand. I accepted—and ended up staying for six and a half years.

A Brand That Changed Everything

That job changed my skin—and my life. I often joke that if I hadn't discovered that brand, I'd have the skin of a rhinoceros. It really was and still is an exceptional skincare brand I'm still using it over 21 years later and it's my main brand in the salon.

As the UK-wide educator (excluding London), I traveled constantly. While the head office was based in London, I rarely stayed put. I was always on the move, suitcase in tow. It was demanding, but so rewarding.

There's something magical about watching someone grasp a new concept, apply it, and succeed. When students passed their exams, I felt genuine pride. I had taught them. They had believed in themselves. And they made it.

The Cost of Constant Movement

But all that travel took its toll. I counted it up one day – I'd lived in ten different homes in as many years . It was exhausting. I longed for stability, for home.

That's when I decided to rent my flat out in Yorkshire and return to Durham and start a family.

Coming Full Circle

One afternoon, I popped into a local hair salon and immediately recognised the owner and head stylist it was someone I'd been visiting on and off since I was 17. That chance meeting turned into the beginning of my business, Beauty Within Durham.

Twelve years ago, I set up my own business in that very salon, just a mile from Durham city centre. And I've never looked back. Since then we have moved , the award winning salon owner , Philip had a new smaller purpose built salon and there are just the of two of us now. Two sole traders doing what we love. Plus the extra member of staff who comes in one or two days a week, Wendy Whippet, Philip's beloved dog, our clients adore her.

More Than Skin Deep

After 33 years in the industry, I've come to realise something: while I may not have become a nurse, I still care for people – just in a different way.

The work I do is deeply personal. During treatments, people open up. They share their stories, their struggles. There's a natural intimacy to this kind of work. You build trust. You build friendship. It becomes a two-way connection.

The Joy Of Mondays

Over the last 12 years as a sole trader, I've been incredibly fortunate. My clients trust me with their skin—and their lives. They ask after my family. They support me in ways I never imagined.

People often groan, "I hate Mondays or I hate my job." But I love Mondays. I genuinely do. I love opening the salon, welcoming familiar faces and meeting new ones. It never gets old.

Because when you love what you do, even Mondays feel like a gift. Don't get wrong I still get nervous when a new client books in or when regulars return as I want them to have the most amazing experience and the best facial or massage they can experience.

Lessons From My Family

When my dad was younger, he was offered a football trial with Darlington FC. But my grandfather told him, "There's no money in that." That mindset – that money should always come first. My parents have always supported do something you love and obviously pays the bills too.

Yes, building a secure future matters. But over time, I've learned that passion and purpose are just as valuable.

This industry can be financially rewarding – but only with the right guidance.

The Power Of Mentorship

When I first started my business, I made plenty of mistakes. I didn't have a "business brain." I even failed maths at school, which is partly why nursing didn't work out – ironic, since my family is full of teachers, including maths teachers!

That gene definitely skipped me.

But then, I found a business mentor. Someone I'd known and trusted for over 20 years. That changed everything. With the right support, I began to see my business clearly. I learned to step back, evaluate, plan. My mentor opened doors for me – introductions, insights, confidence.

If you're starting a business, here's my number-one tip , find an excellent highly recommend business mentor who understands you and your industry . A huge thank you to my business mentor and friend Susan Routledge .With Susan's expertise and guidance I've achieved more than I ever thought possible. I've even won three industry awards in the last three months alone!

The Next Chapter

Now, I'm back in Durham. Grounded. Fulfilled. Excited for what's next.To those just starting out: keep going. It won't always be easy, but if you're led by passion and surrounded by the right people, you can go further than you ever imagined.

Thank you for taking the time to read my story.

Right – enough writing for now. I'm off to sort out my hanging baskets and repot some plants in the garden.

Much love, Rachael x

About Rachael Howard

Rachael Howard is an award winning highly experienced beauty therapist and skincare educator with over 33 years in the industry. Her extensive career has taken her from delivering luxury treatments on board international cruise ships to leading educational rules in the UK , Ireland and the Middle East.

Now settled in back in Durham she owns and works in her business where she specialises in advanced skincare and holistic therapies. Rachael is widely respected for her passion, professionalism and dedication to raising industry standards.

She continues to empower clients through personalised skin care evidence based knowledge and deep rooted belief in the power of wellbeing.

https://www.instagram.com/beautywithindurham

https://www.facebook.com/beautywithindurham

https://beautywithindurham.co.uk

Sunrise

Bernice Robinson

I'm often asked, "How did you learn to blend your beauty therapy skills and weave them into your holistic treatments?"

I reply, "One moment please."

Join me on a transformative journey where experiences in beauty therapy and an inner calling to heal ignited my path and shone a light on an under-developed realm of possibilities. As a natural intuitive, I began to blend beauty therapy with healing techniques into a career that made me feel empowered to radiate vitality and not be scared or shy to be myself and show up. This led me to becoming one of London's sought-after Reiki Masters and energy therapists. I never stopped believing in myself, even when I experienced a few giggles among well-meaning colleagues, all in good fun.

My ten college distinctions over two years in beauty therapy led to my college entering me for the World Skills Live heat in Scotland, where I achieved Silver. It was my commitment to myself and to excellence that defined my path forward.

My story began in beauty therapy, where I spent 20 years crafting treatments to enhance outer and inner beauty. During one particular client's facial, her tears revealed deeper emotional needs, which stimulated my intuition. This planted seeds in my mind that I had not experienced before. I felt a spark to explore the energy that connects body, mind and spirit.

In 2008, a chance encounter with Reiki unveiled my intuitive healing abilities in a treatment that left me cocooned in warmth, as if the universe had whispered 'this is your path.' I wasn't sure what it was, but by 2010 I took a leap of faith, becoming a Reiki Master and teacher. Despite doubts, I continued to believe in my own natural ability and in myself.

My practice blossomed in Mayfair, earning me the title of its best-kept secret. In 2012, I brought intuitive healing to the *X Factor* set, calming contestants' nerves with Reiki and performing deep cleansing facials to get their skin HD ready for filming.

During this time, I also collaborated with the Katie Piper Foundation and worked with Katie, offering beauty therapy and makeup to seriously disfigured women. It was a day of pure joy to see them shine and flow from their transformation. A similar event was organised where I volunteered again, this time for a Fortnum & Mason's ladies' lunch, raising funds for cancer through the Look Good Feel Better campaign.

From 2011 to 2016, my business was thriving and I had a junior therapist working with me. Then suddenly, later in 2016, my mum was diagnosed with Alzheimer's and the bottom fell out of my world. Everything came to a standstill. Fortunately, I had invested well and made the decision to close the business and move home to my parents' in Essex to help my dad care for my mum. I was blessed with amazing parents who always encouraged me to do my best, treat others as I would want to be treated and always be polite and respectful.

Life became difficult for us as a family and, at times, beyond challenging. For the next four years my daily routine was 24/7, seven days a week, but you do get through it. I had to dig deep and find resilience. That inner strength made me stronger.

By 2019, I was invited to become the Reiki Master for the Aman Spa at the Connaught Hotel in Mayfair. I cherished the history of the building. It felt like coming home in a funny kind of way.

Years before, I had experienced Reiki when I hurt my lower back. A pulled muscle released and I was able to stand upright again. I was drawn to understand what had just happened, and eventually trained with a world-renowned Reiki Master in the City of London. I never looked back. I was able to help my mum in many ways, especially calming her down when she felt panicked or alarmed. I'm so thankful I learned this ancient Japanese healing technique, which dates back more than 2000 years and travelled from China through Japan before being brought to the West in the 1890s. We can all learn to heal. We all have the ability.

It's simply a case of learning and then giving.

My amazing mum passed away in May 2020. I felt her energy leave her body as I held her in my arms with my dad. Because I remain open to receiving – with boundaries and protection in place – I still feel her by my side. She is my guiding angel, as is my dear dad, who passed eight months later. I learned that bereavement and grief are life changing. Life would never be the same again. How I got here was gone forever. I felt lost and abandoned. I managed each new day with what little courage I could muster, and I always showed up. I made sure to create precious memories, taking lots of photos and videos. They warm my heart.

I remember my parents saying, "Always be kind and make the most of what you have, because you never know what could happen unexpectedly. You have one life – live it to the fullest." How right they were. I'm doing my best.

During lockdown, I gained further qualifications in holistic life coaching and NLP. I began helping clients break through limiting beliefs by blending these tools with energy work. One lovely client, stuck in self-doubt, felt transformed through NLP. Stepping into her power was a testament to the strength of the mind and subconscious. This was when I created my guided 'White Balloon Meditation', blending a little NLP to release stored emotions.

I always encourage others in our industry not to be afraid to explore the gifts we're all born with. Be brave. Reach out to like-minded people. You can bring something truly special to your treatments and your clients' lives with subtlety and calm.

I trained in Education and Training and am currently developing a course in holistic energy therapies, sharing my intuitive techniques with aspiring healers. Teaching others to shine through their gifts fuels my passion.

Your time to shine is about embracing every experience. Let it inspire you to uncover your own light. Step into the luxury of self-discovery and healing. Explore and go for the sunrise.

Years ago, I toured both islands of New Zealand and visited Rotorua, a land of geothermal wonders. At a beautiful spa nestled in the hot springs, I experienced a coconut and pineapple body scrub using Maori healing traditions. As my skin glowed, I felt a connection to nature's energies. That moment inspired my massage and foot pressure point rituals. Coconut's nourishing essence became my signature, blending ancient wisdom with modern innovation.

Later, I travelled to the Middle East, where the warmth

of Arabian oils and heady scented treatments in a Dubai spa transported me. Healers used nature's gifts to restore balance. I thought deeply about how to bring these elements into my own practice to treat not only facial lines but emotional burdens too, fostering an inner radiance.

I had a similar experience in Bali, where oils are hand-blended based on your treatment. It's a magical place, full of Mother Nature's gifts.

In recent years, I created a healing blend called Reiki Tea®, inspired by many years of listening to clients' stomachs gurgle mid-treatment! I researched calming blends and developed one that soothes digestion and supports relaxation. Reiki Tea® was born.

I've also been working with my local MP to make holistic Reiki treatments available in local hospitals. This is my way of giving back to the incredible industry that has given me so much.

The transition into healing wasn't always easy.

At first, when I verbally offered gentle alternative therapies, however subtly integrated, many clients weren't sure how they could benefit. But over time, as I gradually introduced elements like crystals, sound bowls and my crystal harp for aura cleansing, clients became fascinated and loved the deep relaxation these treatments created.

I was fortunate to be interviewed by Caroline Tell, a New York journalist, while working at Akasha Spa in the Hotel Café Royal. The piece appeared in the New York Times. Jane Knight, travel writer for The Times (UK)*, also experienced a Reiki session with me. At first, she admitted she was sceptical and had wished she'd booked a massage instead. But in her review, she said it gave her the best night's sleep – no small thing given her constant time-zone shifts. Her knee pain, which had persisted despite physio, also completely disappeared.

You never know how deeply healing energy can affect each individual. But it's worth exploring. And training is essential if you wish to gain professional insurance.

I hope my story inspires you to be brave. Stand in your own shoes. Head for that magical place. Live beyond your dreams. And let your inner light shine – like the sunrise.

* Media

https://recommend.com/destinations/europe/wellbeing-specialists-walk-the-walk/

https://www.thetimes.com/travel/destinations/uk-travel/england/london-travel/akasha-holistic-wellbeing-centre-hotel-cafe-royal-piccadilly-london-9vzqd87ps

About Bernice Robinson

Bernice Robinson, founder of Mayfair Holistics & Wellness and the Mayfair Anti-Ageing Studio (est. 2011), is often called Mayfair's best-kept secret.

With 20 years of transformative experience, she blends intuitive alchemy and healing into her signature 90-minute ritual – smoothing facial lines while nurturing inner wellbeing.

A Reiki Master-Teacher, Holistic Life Coach, and NLP practitioner, Bernice empowers clients to shine holistically. She's supported the Katie Piper Foundation and Look Good Feel Better, and also works at the Aman Spa, Connaught Hotel.

With ten college distinctions and a World Skills Live Silver Award, she is now developing a course to inspire beauty professionals to unlock their intuitive gifts. Her philosophy: self-love, self-belief, radiance.

https://www.bernicerobinson.co.uk/

https://www.reikitea.co.uk/

http://linkedin.com/in/bernice-robinson-founder-mayfair-holistics-and-wellness-98935120

https://www.the-connaught.co.uk/aman-spa/aman-spa-treatments/aman-experts/

https://www.instagram.com/reiki_goddess_uk/?hl=en

https://www.the-cma.org.uk/practitioners/bernice-robinson/

I Got There In The End

Kathy Scott

As a little girl one of my favourite games was to comb my dad's very sparse hair and put ribbons in it or to tiptoe into my parents' bedroom to play with the forbidden fruits on my mum's dresser – her purple pot of Cyclax moisturiser, Max Factor face compact and Revlon pink lipstick.

When I was 11, my mum got a part-time job at a hairdressers. During school holidays and Saturdays, I went with her and helped fold the towels, tidy the trolleys or hand the stylists the rollers that created those essential shampoo and sets, or purple rinse perms. Now, there was a look!

I was fascinated by the salon manager, Jackie, a powerhouse of a woman with a steel-grey bob, large glasses, elegant clothes and a desirable postcode.

I unknowingly picked up all sorts of tips about running a salon that I still remember; always have an empty slot in your appointment book to fit in that last-minute person who may turn into a loyal client, keep the salon floor and mirrors spotless, ensure the staff room is clean and tidy, reward your VIP clients, keep to time, wear smart uniforms.

I also had my first taste of the beauty industry – electrolysis, performed by a lady in a crisp, starched white coat and bold makeup, who smoked like a chimney during breaktimes. 1971. Different times.

But I intuitively knew that telling my parents I wanted to train in hair and beauty would have led to a domestic meltdown. That was not the plan my parents had for me. They had come from total poverty in the Gorbals of Glasgow. My mother, a child of Irish Catholic immigrants and equally poor father, saw education, a university degree, and achieving great career heights as the way out. And let's not forget the good Catholic marriage with a brood of children.

Career advice at my Catholic convent school amounted to: become a nurse, go to university, be a teacher, a nun, a wife and a mother. Other choices didn't exist.

I never thought to question or object. But something didn't sit quite right.

It was 34 years before I was able to uncover and express my true intuitive, healing nature within the holistic and beauty world.

In writing this piece, I hope to help you reach your potential far more quickly than I did in this amazing, powerful, important and often undervalued industry.

The Long Way Round

One of the benefits of my upbringing and education, was a strong work ethic, a determination and a willingness to constantly learn and improve. I was always asking questions, looking for opportunities to expand my knowledge and skills. I'd gone a long way in a career in Human Resources, but I realised I was bored and undervalued.

There was no point in looking for other jobs, climbing the ladder further, battling male prejudice. It just didn't appeal, despite being offered a Deputy Directorship in an even bigger multinational company with a career path to Director. That would have secured a very comfortable financial future, and I'd probably have retired ten years ago.

But my body had other plans. In my childhood I had several accidents that affected my spine. As I progressed in HR, my health began to decline. Nothing major, but persistent enough to become a problem. Someone suggested I visit an osteopath. I walked into that clinic in pain and discomfort. I walked out with a body that felt free and at ease.

My path to re-training in alternative and holistic therapies was ignited.

When Love And Skill Meet

'When love and skill work together, expect a masterpiece',
John Ruskin.

There are so many different disciplines within our industry. Are you drawn to one over another? Do you think it's time to niche your business? If you know your magic, what sets you alight, then focus on that.

Touch therapies were my heart and soul. However, I also wanted to expand my knowledge and moved into advanced skin science. There was so much to learn. Aesthetics didn't align with my philosophy of life and ageing. The training costs outweighed the financial benefits I could expect, given the years I had left as an active therapist.

I asked myself the question: if I had to do one thing day in day out, what would it be? The answer - facials.

I brought the two sides together, to create my USP: Renewed Spirit - Radiant Skin. The combination of touch, non-invasive technology, problem solving, skin science, brand relationships, ingredient research and creating moments of bliss in a divine environment, just ticks all my boxes – brain, hands, heart and soul.

By focusing on my magic, I've created a workplace and business that feeds me emotionally, intellectually and spiritually. I work from a beautiful, peaceful space where the client experience starts the moment, they turn up the driveway. I attract clients who value what I do. I help people. I support them as they journey along their own path to better health and inner peace. I feel fulfilled.

What gets you going? Investigate that. You don't have to do everything. But you do need to do what you love and value.

Mind The Gap

It's an understatement to say I'm not numerate. I started my salon with no outside support to offset my missing skills. It was the start of a whole new journey when I realised, I needed help. Whether it's business planning, finances, marketing, or digital tools, get help in whatever area is not your strength.

More than that, join support groups, masterminds, business development classes, attend free training sessions, go to shows, enter awards, read books and industry magazines. These things broaden your mind, expand your contacts and increase your opportunities to collaborate.

This book, along with the two preceding it, is a clear example of what I'm talking about. Connection is everything. Don't isolate yourself. Remember, you don't have to do it all at once.

Trust Your Intuition

If I had trusted my intuition sooner in life, I would have reached my sweet spot much more easily, avoided unhealthy situations, and saved myself pain. We are all intuitive beings. In this industry, especially in holistic therapies, it's vital we learn to listen to and develop that inner knowing. If something feels wrong, it usually is. If something keeps calling you, don't ignore it.

Ask The Questions Others Avoid

I heard someone say recently that when they considered making a life change, their friends and family told them, "Don't think about that, just wait and you'll see it's all going to be OK."

What a terrible thing to say to someone who wants to reflect on how they got to a place of unhappiness. But fear kicks in - not yours, theirs - and they want you to maintain the status quo. That's why they sidetrack you.

Not asking the questions and ignoring your thoughts and feelings leads to stagnation, frustration and missed opportunities, which will eventually take its toll on you.

So don't be afraid to stop, ask, explore, change and grow.

You're So Lucky

As Henry Ford said, 'The harder I work, the luckier I get'. Even further back, Seneca said "Luck is what happens when preparation meets opportunity".

People have said to me, "You're so lucky to work for yourself. You've such a beautiful salon you're so lucky. Aren't you lucky to work in such a lovely space. You're so lucky to have loyal clients."

No. It wasn't luck. It was choices, education, effort, investment, failure, self-development, being alert to opportunities, and most of all persistence. If this sounds like you, be proud of the luck you have created for yourself and don't let anyone tell you otherwise.

If You Can't Find It, Create It

Some of us are leaders. Some are followers. Some love being in a team. Some prefer to be alone. There are plenty of personality tests that reveal our natural tendencies. But either way, you have agency.

What kind of environment do you need to thrive? What kind of working style do you need? What does success mean to you? What does your best business look like?

When I shared my business idea with someone. Their reply? "That's just pie in the sky." Funny that, Ginger Tree celebrates its 20th anniversary in 2025. I made it happen.

Even now, I am developing new ideas – a coaching model, a book and a training course designed specifically for holistic therapists. These are born from a deep love for this work and a genuine desire to share what I have learned along the way.

If the support or business doesn't exist for you right now, create it, whether it's a unique treatment approach, a brand, a community, or a philosophy. You are free to invent your own rules and build a business that perfectly expresses your authentic self.

Closing Thoughts: Contentment Is Underrated

Success doesn't have to be flashy. It doesn't need to be loud. Quiet contentment – waking up knowing you are aligned, fulfilled, and free – is a beautiful goal.

Wherever you are in your beauty business journey, keep going. Stay curious. Ask for help. Follow your magic.

You don't need to wait 34 years to feel at home in your skin, your business and your soul.

About Kathy Scott

Kathy Scott is a multi-award-winning holistic skin practitioner with over 30 years' experience at the forefront of integrative skin health. Following a successful corporate career in HR, leadership development and team facilitation, Kathy retrained as a homeopath and went onto build a thriving salon business grounded in natural, non-invasive skin therapies. Her progressive approach combines clinical results with deep therapeutic care. A lifelong learner and innovator, Kathy is now a qualified Trauma-Informed Nervous System Coach with Nicole Gomez. She is also a BABTAC Ambassador, a member of the Beauty Director's Club, and a sought-after speaker, judge, and author within the industry. Passionate about raising standards in holistic beauty, Kathy has held the prestigious PHAB Service Stars Award for three consecutive years. She is currently writing a book and developing a training programme to support fellow holistic therapists in delivering results-driven, heart-led treatments.

@gingertreebeauty

www.gingertreebeauty.co.uk

kathy@gingertreeskinclinic.co.uk

Beauty & The Best 1 & 2

If you loved *Beauty & The Best 3*, please find *Beauty & The Best* books *1* and 2 on Amazon globally in both digital and paperback.

Printed in Dunstable, United Kingdom

66536864R00109